Enduring Life Pitfalls

By

C K King

Published by New Generation Publishing in 2022

Copyright © C K King 2022

First Edition

The author asserts the moral right under the Copyright, Designs and Patents Act 1988 to be identified as the author of this work.

All Rights reserved. No part of this publication may be reproduced, stored in a retrieval system or transmitted, in any form or by any means without the prior consent of the author, nor be otherwise circulated in any form of binding or cover other than that which it is published and without a similar condition being imposed on the subsequent purchaser.

ISBN
    Paperback   978-1-80369-413-9
    Hardback   978-1-80369-414-6
    Ebook   978-1-80369-415-3

www.newgeneration-publishing.com

 New Generation Publishing

Preface

With a childhood which was like swimming against the tidal current, in a dysfunctional parental setting, where both parents dedicated most of their time to their work and their social life, Christiana was left to look after herself around age eight. By nine years old, she became the primary carer to her father when he suddenly got sick. After the death of her father, and going through an eleven-year civil war Christiana had to find her way in the city of Freetown age sixteen. It was time for Christiana to fall in love with yet more family heartache. It was then that she stumbled into her long-lost childhood sweetheart and decided to move to the UK with him. Would it finally be calm waters for Christiana, or was it the beginning of more of life's pitfalls?

By C K King

11 March 2022

Chapter 1

A man stood on the steps of Kambia hospital, on a dark Christmas night, shouting, "My wife has just delivered, it's a girl and her name is Christiana." That man was my father. He had been drinking and celebrating with friends during that Christmas day. My mother told me this same story every year around my birthday. "This child is going to be born on Christmas day as long as he or she is my child, they will be born on Christmas day," my father would say to her repeatedly. She told me my father moved to Kambia immediately after he graduated from college or university. That was when he met my mother. My mother said she got married to my father at a young age, around nineteen years old. She also told me her mother died when they were young. My grandmother from my mother gave birth to six children, two girls and four boys, her father remarried and they were brought up by their stepmother. I knew from her own narration it was not a smooth relationship between them and their stepmother when my mother got married to my father.

By the time I was born, she had already had a number of miscarriages, about three of them. Because I was the first one to be born, my grandparents named me Synkortho. In the Limba language it means, "we will soon know the reason, or all will be revealed". A phrase or a sentence can have slightly different meaning in my place. Synkortho was also the name of my grandmother, my father's mother, one of the wives of the paramount chief of the Kasonko chiefdom. He was very pleased for his first son to finally have a child, or for him to hold the grandchild of his first son, I was told.

Soon after my birth, both of my parents moved to another town, Magburaka. My father worked as a teacher while my mother trained as a midwife community healthcare nurse. That was my first relocation. Within three years my younger brothers arrived. Twins, both of them were boys, but only one of them survived. My mother was also a twin, a fraternal twin. My younger brother was named after my grandfather. It was a long name but we simply called him Baio or Pa Baio. As a young boy he was always so full of life, positive energies, really active and everyone adored him.

We lived in two bedrooms in a compound setting.

It was at the end of a warm sunny day, in the dry season, which is like the summer season, when a tall girl walked in with my father, she was clutching a small bag containing her clothes or belongings. She was around the same age as me, around six or six and a half years old or maybe a little more. I immediately stood up to greet them. She had one of the brightest smiles I have ever seen. *E black dae shine*, as we say in our local dialect, meaning "her dark skin tone glows". I was immediately drawn to her.

"This is Fudia, my younger sister's daughter, she is your cousin and will be staying with us from now on." My father introduced her. She smiled again and shook my hand which was already extended. "Kushe, Na me name Christiana, everyone calls me Mormi." I introduced myself. Mormi was what every family member and close friends called me when I was growing up. Fudia greeted my brother, mother and all the uncles and aunties. My mother showed her where to put her bag and just like that it was like she had always been in the family. There was no rivalry or anything of the sort between us; finally, someone to share the same interest with. I had been blessed with a sister.

My brother spent a lot of time with the other men in the family. There was Uncle Jibrila, Edward and Brima, whom he always hung around and played with. Now I got to spend time with Fudia endlessly and not just with the boys or men in the family. I had a lot of friends within the compound houses. My friend Isatu was a bit older than I was, she lived with her older sister and her husband. Isatu had told me she was going back to the village in a couple of years because her parents had already accepted her bride price for her. She was to be the third wife of some man in their village. Ya-ester and Alice were also close friends of mine but their grandmother, whom they lived with, did not let them stay outside for too long. She always called them back inside immediately it started to turn dark. They had lost their mother a while back. I didn't really know how their mother had died but that was the reason they were living with their grandmother. They were never allowed to play out with the other children for too long. Now I didn't just have to be around my mother and her friends in the evenings, or with the uncles or Baio and their friends, Fudia would be there too.

We liked being around the grown-ups because they always told stories and jokes every evening when they gathered around. Sometimes the stories could be really scary; it was good to have Fudia because we could just leave and play on our own if the stories got much too scary to listen to.

From that moment on we were inseparable, we played together, went to fetch water together, ate together, helped in the kitchen together and washed all the pots and pans together. Washing up before and after cooking was something I never looked forward to. At least now there was another helping hand to make it a less daunting task. Staying in and around the kitchen was a must when growing up because that was how you learnt the fundamentals of cooking. That was what my mother and all grown-ups used to say. They would say things like, "You have to be able to cook well for your husband when you get married. It is a horror, if your husband is not able to eat what you cooked."

Things changed when my father came home one evening and announced to us that we would be starting school in the coming week. It was on a weekend; he showed us our uniforms and everything we needed for school. He said we would be attending the Roman Catholic school for girls. (RC Girls for short.) I did not know what to expect as I had never been to a school or inside a classroom before. On Sunday evening, we washed our hair and Cisi asked one of the older aunties to braid our hair for us. The uniforms were ironed. Everything was ready on Sunday evening. You could not leave the ironing until Monday morning because the coal goose iron took too long to warm up. Cisi was my biological mother, but we all called her Cisi because that was what everyone called her when we were growing up. And we called our father Uncle for the same reasons.

On Monday morning we woke up early to eat breakfast and get ready for school. From our home to school it was about a two to three miles' walk or maybe more. My father carried me on his head all the way to the school while holding Fudia's hand. We walked in silence all the way to the school. It was a big school with different buildings within reach. There were buildings for lower classrooms and higher classrooms. We approached one of the buildings and stopped at one of the doors, the door was partly open. A woman was writing with chalk on the blackboard. Children were sitting on little chairs and tables.

They were writing on their papers what the teacher was writing on the blackboard. The teacher immediately stopped writing and came to the door to greet us. She spoke to my father for a few minutes and then knelt down so she could look at us in the face directly. She spoke to me and Fudia, "What are your names?" and looked from Fudia to me or the reverse. We responded and gave her our names. She welcomed us, spoke to my father briefly, and with a wave my father was gone. The teacher escorted us and showed us our seats. Everyone in the classroom was paying attention as we took our seats. It was a nervous and uncomfortable feeling.

Mrs Bangura, as she introduced herself, gave us some A4 papers, pencils and crayons. She asked us to draw what was on the board and colour it with a colour of our choice. As we did so all the other children focused back on their work, then I felt less uncomfortable. After some time, the bell rang, it was break time, we went outside to have our break. Our break was spent chatting to the other children. Just like that we were playing and interacting with one another. By the end of the school day Uncle came to pick us.

This time he walked before us as Fudia and I followed him in silence. That was our first day of school and that was our routine for the first few days. By the end of the week, we knew the route to school, and it was only us who walked to and fro from school. The road was straight forward. There was no reason for us to be scared because so many other children walked the same route to school every day.

Chapter 2

About two weeks later, we arrived to an empty house, there were no mother, father or any of the uncles and aunties anywhere. That was just how it was, no one told you anything or notified you about anything, and as a child you were not allowed to ask a lot of questions, or it could be construed as rude to question an adult. But there was always that uncle or aunty who you could talk to and ask as many questions as you liked. One of them for me was Uncle Gibrila, he would tell us precisely what was going on. I went searching for him and he was sat on a neighbour's balcony just opposite to ours.

In our discussion he explained that Cisi had started training at the hospital and my father had gone to Rowgbonm with his friends. He went on to explain that Uncle Brima had also started working at Margbass. Rowgbom was like a pub. As I later found out, people from various walks of life went there on a regular basis to socialise, eat local delicacies, drink beverages, drink alcohol and smoke cigarettes. And Margbass was a company which mainly transformed the sugar cane into sugar and into various forms of spirit alcohol.

We ate our food and did our chores as usual.

From then on, I started to be aware of a shift, things were pulling in different directions. You could tell a change had crept in; you could certainly feel it. My father would come home very late at night because he went from working to socialising, and by the time he got home it was always very late at night. Most times he would not even eat his food, he would just go straight to bed. My mother was hardly at home, she was now training on the job, she was doing long hours almost every day including weekends. She was doing three days and three nights at the government hospital. She was also spending most of her time with the other women on the course while doing coursework. My mother would sleep during the day after the long night shifts. Tension began to build up between my mother and father, the tension was unhidden, you could see it, you could almost touch it. The snapping, arguments and fighting had become an everyday recurrence. The less time my father saw my mother the more he stayed out. Any chance of them being in the house together was worrying for us because they would end up arguing. It got so bad that all the neighbours in the compound and outside the compound would come outside, some would stand around, while some watched from their windows and others would come between them trying to separate them. When the big fights began, the crowd got bigger as everyone watched or tried to dissolve the issue, or tried to find a solution to their issues. All I wanted to do was run and hide, the embarrassment was too much, especially when some of my friends were also watching. I could not look them in the face. It became some sort of drama series between them. One day as soon as my mother entered the house, my father attacked her with a set of long whips which I saw him put behind the sofa.

    They were freshly cut because the leaves were still fresh on them. I had no idea what he was going to do with them. He was in one of those moods which told you to keep away and ask no questions if you knew what was good for you. When my mother came into the living room, which we called the parlour, and sat on that same sofa, my father removed the little canes or sticks or whips from where he had put them and started striking my mother everywhere.

He hit her on the head, the back, the arms, it was very unexpected for her, and for us. As she screamed and shouted in agony, we were crying too. There was nothing much we could do except call out for him to stop. "Uncle lef am, lef am," we shouted in Krio. Baio was crying his eyes out. He did not stop, he just carried on beating her. Fudia somehow managed to stand in front of my mother; that was when he stopped and my mother had a chance to run outside. There were marks and blisters all over her body. By the time Uncle Brima jumped from his balcony to ask what was going on everything was over. Uncle Brima started talking to my father in their language. You could tell he was not pleased with his actions.

A few people went to console my mother. I went to bed and curled myself up so hard, all I wanted to do at that moment was disappear. I didn't know which one was worse: the pain my mother was going through, not being able to do anything, or the fact that everyone was watching. I heard Fudia calling me when it was all over, but I did not respond. I was in no mood to see anyone or speak to anyone let alone play games or listen to any stories on that day. Other husbands and wives did have fights and quarrels from time to time, but it was not as intense and regular as my mother and father.

"Mormi, mormi, wake up," Fudia called and tapped me on the arm early morning. "Wake up, let's go and fetch water before everyone gets there." If you didn't go first thing in the morning the water would be dirty. If you wanted clean water to drink and wash you had to be there first thing in the morning. It was not that far but the road had some rocks and trees on the way. And the roots of some of the trees cut across the road which made the water shake and splash from the bucket as you walked up and down the hilly road. Most times you would have a full bucket of water on your head and by the time you got home it was half full. We had two drums to fill before we went to school. That was our number-one task every day except if it rained some nights, then we would wake up to full drums of water. After the water fiasco, we then turned our attention to making our own breakfast before we set off for school. All three of us walked to school together.

The boys school was just next to the girls school. We went together most times and came back together, except if Baio decided to walk with his friend Daddy-Sambo which he did sometimes. When we came home one day, as we get closer to the house, I could hear my mother's voice from a distance. When she was around you knew she was around because she was usually teasing someone, laughing loudly or she was busy telling jokes. If you did anything she did not agree with, my mother would tell you about it there and then, or simply tell you off. Most people I knew liked to be around my mother. When we arrived, everything looked fine; it had been a long time since she had been home when we returned from school. She was cooking on both of the stoves, the small one for the *plasas*, that is the source, and the big stove for the rice. The wood was dry, both fires were blazing. We quickly got out of our school uniforms, put on house clothes and went to help out in the kitchen. We knew our roles, which were to beat peppers, onions and all the ingredients for the plasas, and to wash the dishes.

Everything was running smoothly. Before we knew it, we were eating our food. Oh, how I wish it was like this every day I said to myself as we ate. When we finished eating, my mother had a wash and a change of clothes while we put everything back where it was supposed to be. The two stoves were still outside because they had to cool down before we could put them back. As we sat on the veranda with freshly stuffed tummies, playing and laughing, I saw my father casually walking home. It was just starting to turn dark, but you could never miss his tall and slender appearance. We greeted him, he nodded, went in, and put his papers, books, or whatever stuff he always carried, in his portfolio or briefcase. My mother was inside the house when my father got in. I have no idea what transpired between them.

All I saw was my mother rushing outside, and my father following her from behind. Before I could make out what was going on, my mother grabbed the small stove and threw it towards my father, it missed him, my father grabbed the same stove and sent it back at my mother, and it landed on my mother's forehead. She tried to move but she could not, there was blood flowing down her face like someone had opened a tap. The blood was everywhere, she could not see where she was going. By this time the place was packed with people. I saw the people from the compound had come to watch what was going on as my mother tried to climb the steps on the veranda calling for me, Baio and Fudia. The blood was oozing so fast and it had covered her face and it was on her chest.

Then she fell. I saw her go down like a bag of sack. She lay down motionless on the concrete floor, she was on her back. The three of us were also crying as we watched. We moved closer and stood over her. I thought she was dead. Uncle Brima sent one of the boys to go and call a taxi, some of the people were trying to stop the bleeding, some were fanning her, and others were pouring water on her. One of them was saying she had fainted. She was helped into the taxi and taken to the hospital for treatment. They kept her overnight and stitched her head. She returned the following day with eight or more stitches; I cannot remember exactly.

The commotion subsided a bit after their last fight and things appeared to be calm. I was not sure if it was a conscious decision but they both did their parts to avoid one another. If one of them was coming home, it was time for the other one to go to work and that was the way it was most of the time. My father would finish from work and head straight to socialise with his friends, he would come home very late at night or when we were already asleep. He hardly touched his food. He would come home and just crash on the sofa with his shirt and shoes still on.

My mother spent all her time in hospital or slept off those night shifts, or spent time with her friends. I asked myself the same question so many times. Why can't they just get along, the non-stop fights between them have to stop? I sometimes longed for them to be at home together, at the same time, but in reality I prefered them not to be.

At least this way they were not trying to, or killing one another, or gathering a crowed. My mother had become withdrawn from almost everyone and from us too as I noticed the difference in her personality. It was like she did not want to be in that house or be there with us anymore. She snapped, yelled, called me names and was frequently in a bad mood. She always had a reason to leave the house, there was always something she had got to do.

Chapter 3

It was time for the long holidays. Whenever we had a long break from school, it was usually for about six weeks or more. It was also the time when you got promoted to another class. If you did well, you moved to another class with all of your friends and if you did not meet the required criteria you would stay in the same class. No one wanted to do that or wanted that to happen to them. We were happy to have passed our exams and got to go to another class with all the other children. We had come to know some of them really well. We played together at school and walked home together.

Holding our results, which were also called report cards, in our hands, we handed them to my father. Later that week, he told us that we were going to spend the holidays with his mother. I had seen pictures where my late grandfather was holding me and pictures of me and my grandmother together, but I had no recollection of those pictures. And sometimes some members of the family would come to visit us and they brought with them all kinds of freshly harvested produce. Some of it would be from their farms and some from their gardens. This was going to be the first time I would get to meet and know my grandmother with some of the extended members of the family. My mother was not coming with us because she was doing her practical or practice in a town called Mashengbin.

I was secretly counting the days to our departure. I had loved everyone who had come to visit us and now I would get to visit them and meet my grandmother, uncles, cousins and everyone else.

We woke up early morning to pack our bags, get dressed, have something to eat and then we were on our way. The four of us walked all the way to the car park at Magburaka town centre. We entered a small car heading to Makeni. When we got to Makeni, the driver dropped us off at another car park, a similar setting to the car park we had just left, but this car park was bigger, busier and nosier. My father paid the driver and we proceeded to another car. As we approached the car, I could hear the apprentice shouting, "Fadugu! Fadugu! Fadugu!" The apprentice was a driver's assistant. They found all the passengers for the car, helped to load their luggage, and in some cases, even collected the fares from the passengers and then gave them to the driver. The drivers just drove the car after the apprentice had filled it with the required passengers. That was one of the ways they learnt the trade of becoming a driver themselves. As my father negotiated the fare for the four of us, I noticed that this vehicle was much bigger than the one that had just brought us. It was like a van with strong metal roof racks to carry the luggage on top.

There were bags of rice, sugar, salt being loaded on top of the roof rack. Inside the van there were three straight long benches, one on each side and one in the middle. It was a high van; the apprentice had to help us up. We were sitting so close together you could barely move your arms and legs. Only when the van had been crammed packed to its fullest capacity, that was when I saw a man talking to the apprentice. They had a few exchanges between them and he took to the driver's seat. He was obviously the driver of the van. A few moments later we left Makeni heading towards Fadugu.

We passed a lot of small towns and villages on the way, that was all I could remember, and then suddenly we were jolted to a stop. I must have slept as I usually dozed whenever I was on a long journey. The apprentice announced that they were going to stop for a couple of minutes. He said we could all get off and go for a toilet break then return back to the vehicle in a couple of minutes. This quick stop was absolutely needed I thought to myself. We could at least get some fresh air and straighten our legs. It was really hot inside the car. When we got down, I was shocked by the size of the township. It was called Binkorlo and they were selling all kinds of freshly prepared produce on the roadside. There was also a toilet for you to use, which we took turns to do. As I saw my father standing at a small food stall by the roadside, my stomach automatically started to do acrobatics. I had not eaten anything since morning and it must have been late afternoon, told by the strength of the sun. My father bought us some roast corn, pealed oranges and *parch granat*. Parch granat were roasted salted peanuts. He also got us some plastic water. The salt on the hot peanuts tasted really good, it was delicious. We had just started eating when the driver returned and the apprentice shouted, "Everybody cam load mek we dae go. Everyone on board we have to get going." Because we were children, we had to get in first. We found a way to finish them inside that cramped car because there was no way I was throwing the food away. Very soon we were moving again. The car travelled for a long time before it started to slow down. I could hear the voice of the apprentice coming from the roof of the car. He had packed the car so much that he had not even left a place for himself to sit on. He had to sit on top of the van with all the luggage. The apprentice told us that some of the men and women would have to come down as the car was struggling to climb the hill. Looking through the window it was fascinating and scary at once. It was the SS Curve; I had heard so much about it from the uncles and aunties who had visited us. They told us stories about how dangerous it was and how accidents happened there frequently.

The SS Curve was a hill that was shaped like the letter S because it was so long and because of the way it was laid out. I am sure that is why they called it the SS Curve. Most of the grown-ups got out of the car and they walked behind it slowly. The view from my seat was clearer now I could see where we were heading to, and it certainly looked like an S. The scariest part for me was the cuts in the side of the hills. We were now so very high you could see how steep it was when you looked down. There was hardly anything to block the car should anything happen. Fudia and I just looked at each other. Baio was still sleeping beside Fudia and my father was sitting at the front with the driver. After a short while the car stopped to wait for the other passengers as they got back into the car. We had passed the dangerous parts of the hill.

Chapter 4

Once more it was the voice of the apprentice which woke me up. He was urging everyone to pay their fares. We had finally arrived in Fadugu, my limbs felt weak from sitting for so long. Bags collected, we followed our father across the road. As we approached my grandfather's house, which was situated at the centre of the town, some family members came rushing towards us. I could hear some of them saying, "Den don cam," meaning "They are here".

It was like they were expecting us, maybe Uncle had sent a message about our visit I thought. The place was already turning dark, it must have been late in the evening. The veranda was packed with people. Pafinoh, the then section chief, after the death of my grandfather, was sitting at the far end on what looked like a rocking chair with an arm rest. Beside him were large jugs of *bulee* with *poyo* or palm wine that were slowly froshing and flowing away. Everyone else sat on a long bench within reach of one another. The bulee was a traditional container used mostly for storing and transporting palm wine also known as poyo. We greeted the elders, slightly bending the knees as a sign of respect. In the living room my grandmother and all the elderly women were sitting down. My grandmother was sitting just by the door as we walked in. She looked at my father and called my father by his traditional name, Borbor. My father smiled slightly and said, "Innah," then they exchanged some sort of greetings in the Limba language. I later find out that Borbor was what all the elders called him, even my grandmother was called Narda-Borbor, which meant the mother of Borbor. After greeting all the men on the veranda, it was now time to greet all the women in the parlour: Mami Nancy, Mami Iye, Marie Mansary, Cici Nancy, Nada Sali and so many others. When the greeting session was over, grama finally took us to her room or little apartment. It was also packed with cousins, Mummy Kay, Niyo, Nayomi, Abie and Musu. They were all chatting, arguing, laughing and playing. God, every room we had entered so far had been packed with people I said to myself.

After a quick interaction and exchanges, we entered another door, and you could tell it was my grandmother's room. It had a large bed and a large table. By the end of the bed, at the foot was a huge window, big enough for two people to pass through it at the same time. We put our bags down and as she sat on the bed she gestured for us to sit down beside her. She looked at us with the most loving and compassionate face I had ever seen. Then just like that every little apprehension I may have had just melted away. She spoke in the Limba language, but I could only pick up a few words, which I had learnt from other family members and from my father. We just looked at each other, nodded our heads and smiled. To which she replied, "Una get for learn for talk pa Limba quick." She was saying, "We have to learn to speak in Limba fast."

I was glad and surprised to hear her speak in Krio. Krio was the broken English which almost everyone in the country could speak, there was no language barrier. It was getting peach dark by now, she ruffled around the table, picked something up and then lit the lamp. She put food, which was already on the table, on a plate. "Una cam eat," she told us. We sat around the table and ate. It was rice and it was still hot. "They must have prepared it not long ago," I said as we ate. As soon as we had finished, she gave us some soap and asked Niyo, one of her younger sister's daughters, to show us where we could have a wash.

Fudia and I followed Niyo through the back door and just by the side of the house there was a tap with running water. It was completely perplexing because in Magburaka, which was a bigger town than Fadugu, we had to go and fetch water almost every day and here there was water on the doorsteps. As we started to wash, I asked Niyo why the whole house was packed with so many people. "Is it always like this?"

She said, "It is usually a busy house, but today someone has come to ask for one of the girl's hands in marriage," she explained, "that is why the men are gathered on the veranda and the women are in the living room."

I said again, "You have to get used to it because tomorrow they might come with a dispute to be settled or another one could be getting married," she replied.

"Pass me the soap," Fudia called out. We washed and returned to our grandmother's bedroom. Baio was nowhere to be seen. He must be with our father I supposed. The three of us slept on the bed, Fudia at the back, me in the middle and my grandmother in front.

I woke up to a lot of footsteps, talking and yelling. It was coming from the direction of the big window. Grandma was no longer in the bed and Fudia was still sleeping. I walked to the window and stood there watching. It was a huge backyard. The kitchen faced the back of the house. It was similar to the one in Magburaka but bigger. It had the same structure; there were about four fireplaces going on at the same time. I could see my grandmother stirring something in the pot. She must be making breakfast, maybe. The other women were also busy with their own pots or their own fireplaces.

By the side of the kitchen was a group of girls, some slightly older than I was, some about the same age as me. They were pounding on a very big wooden mortar with a wooden pestle, some were doing it in twos, others in threes and they were singing, some talking at the same time. They were pounding palm canals, which were used to produce palm oil. I could not take my eyes off them. It looked like hard work and it also looked like fun. I had used the wooden mortar and mortar pencil before but only to pound peppers and onions, and it was not as big as the one they were using.

My grandmother saw me at the window as she came to collect something from a huge large wooden box. The box was situated right beneath the window. It was called a chop box: a chop box is where they put dried food and other food items for safekeeping. It may contain things like rice, palm oil, *maggi*, dried fish or dried vegetables. "You are awake," she said to me as she opened the box.

"Good morning granny," I greeted her. She responded with the warmest smile. "Go and wake Fudia up, wash your faces, greet the elders and come eat something, look the food it is almost ready." She pointed at the fireplace which seemed to be dying down. She took something out of the box and returned to the kitchen. I woke Fudia up, we followed the same route to where the tap was. When we finished washing our faces, we met my grandmother in the kitchen and we greeted everyone that was present. Before you spoke to the elders or grown-ups you must greet them first or it was considered to be rude or bad manners. Fudia and I watched as she put some food on one plate or tray and put some stew in the bowl. She then put everything on a larger tray and said "Let's go." We followed her past the women and girls who were doing the pounding. They were so busy I was not sure if they even noticed us. There was another long building by the left side of the main house, it contained about four or five rooms and a parlour. Grandmother entered the last room of the back house and we followed her inside. My father and Baio were sitting on wooden chairs. "So this is where you disappeared to," I spoke as I saw them.

"I stay here every time I am in town," Uncle responded. As my grandmother was putting the food on the table, she said, "I only stayed in town today because of you, as soon as you have settled down I am going to the farm, the others have already left." Oh, that must be why Niyo and the others are nowhere to be found this morning, they must have left for the farm.

"Am coming with you granny," I said,

"Are you sure, getting there is a bit far and the road is difficult to walk on?" my grandmother answered.

"I want to come with you," I replied firmly. She nodded and left the living room. I had not been to a farm before but if my grandmother and the other girls were there, why would I want to stay in the township all day.

Granny said they would only return from the farm late in the evening or sometime at night. Baio and my father said they were going to see the palm trees garden. Fudia said she wanted to stay in town and might come some other time. "Right, we have to get going now, am already late." I followed my grandmother as she led a narrow way from the back of the house. We had just taken a few steps when I heard yelling behind us, "Wait for me." It was Fudia.

The three of us continued walking, as we went on, some of the tree branches would hit us on the arms or even on our faces. "Look where you are going and be careful, parts of the road are slippery," advised my grandmother. I could hear muffled sounds from a distance, we must have been getting closer. We walked a few more minutes before we arrived at the farm. There was a small farmhouse with firewood burning inside of it. Niyo and Nayomi looked surprised but pleased to see us.

We exchanged a quick pleasantry and Nayomi said, "What are you doing here, as if you will be able to do anything on the swamp?" she said teasingly.

"Leave them alone," said Niyo. I had helped my father so many times planting vegetables in a small patch of land at Magburaka, but this was entirely different I said to myself.

Just a few steps away from the hut, or farmhouse, was an open space: it was the swamp, it was long and wide, it had been brushed, the grass burnt down and cleared up. There were a lot of men, some young and some much older, they were holding hoes on their hands, they were using the hoes for digging and tilting the soil. Another group of men were beating on the drums while singing. Their job was to keep the workers motivated and entertained. The workers were so focused and so hard-working it was as if they did not even notice the mild rain.

"This work needs to be finished soon, I have already arranged for the women to come and do the planting of rice, if these men don't finish today or at least do the majority of the work, I could lose the date which the women have given to me. If I lost that date, there is no guarantee on when I could be able to get another date," my grandmother explained and carried on talking. "They have taken up a lot of different farms to work on. The rice has to be planted at the right time." She concluded, "I think they will finish working on it today, look at the way they are going at it really fast."

I answered, "Hope they continue like that; they might slow down as the day goes on especially after having their meals and drinks."

She looked around again and said, "Come we have to start the cooking; they must eat by noon or there will be trouble." The four of us left to go and get some cooking items, we passed through plenty of plants and all kind of fruits and vegetables. Some of the fruits were already ripe on the trees and they were within our reach.

We got the cassava leaves, peppers, aubergine, which we called *corborcorbor*. We got ourselves a few fruits which we ate as we walked back to the farm hut. When we got back to the farm, it was full of women. Large pots were already on the fire, two huge pots were already boiling up. Other family members would usually leave their own farms to help out when they were doing that kind of work for anyone. This was because there was a lot of work to be done. When it was the turn for another person the favour was returned. It was a very busy day and everyone was moving with such a fast pace. Some just knew what to do, others were given and taking instructions. In a couple of hours, the cooking was over. The rain had stopped, the food was dished out in several *bafpans*. A bafpan was a large bowl usually made out of sill. The men, whose job it was to entertain, were notified, they started drumming slowly with a slow song. The workers knew it was time for their dinner because they all started coming in little groups. They came and sat down surrounding the baf-pan with food as they ate in silence. Everyone was silent because it was a sign of respect for the cooks. It was considered to be rude when you spoke and ate at the same time or disrespectful to the cooks.

By the time they finished eating, two men appeared carrying jugs of palm wine over their shoulders. It was fresh from the palm trees, tapped on the day. The men gave out a loud cheer as they finished eating and welcomed the palm wine. As soon as they finished washing their hands, they started serving the palm wine. As they got into it, we finally sat down to eat our own food. Some of the women ate in a small size baf-pan and some from the cooking pot itself. The food tasted great, the men drank, hung around a bit and then got back to work. The women were offered some palm wine also. As they received the palm wine on their hands, they would kneel down to drink the wine. This was also a sign of respect for the men who tapped the palm wine. I saw my grandmother standing at a distance watching as the men continued to work on the swamp, which we also called *portorportor*.

I walked up to her and stood close by her side. She looked at me and I said, "They have not slowed down that much granny."

She replied, "We might be in luck," and smiled.

"I think they are going to finish the work today," said Fudia. We stood there for a while just watching the men. We returned back to the farm where the packing process was in progress. The pots and pans were being washed and packed away, the fireplace was being put out and some of the women were already saying their goodbyes. My grandmother thanked them as they left. Then she turned to us and said, "It is time for you to get going as well, the sun is going down and it might rain again, I don't want you to walk in the dark." Niyo who was the eldest of us all led us back to town. My grandmother stayed back with a few of the women. I really wanted to stay and see if the men would finish the work, but my grandmother insisted on us leaving before it got dark. On our way I noticed we branched on another path halfway on the walk back home. "Where are we going?" asked Fudia.

"To the river," answered Nayomi, "we are having a wash on the way." What they meant was a swim. By the time Fudia and I could say anything they were running, and we were running after them. My God there it was, the river, girls about our age were already in the water, some washing, and others washing their clothes. Before I could say a word Niyo took her clothes off and with only her underwear she jumped into the river and Nayomi followed in, both of them making a big splash. We stood there looking in amazement.

They started shouting and laughing, "Jump in! Come on jump in!" We were still looking at each other. "You will be fine, this area is not that deep." By the time I could say another word, Fudia was already in the water. I took my clothes off and held my nose tightly as I saw they had done when they were jumping in. "You hold your nose to prevent the water going up your nostrils," they said. I hit the water like lead which was a little bit painful. With both eyes closed I was under the water, everything fell silent for a moment and I found myself coming up again, floating and gasping for air. "You see, it is not that bad is it," said Niyo as she splashed the water towards me. I said nothing, that was my first experience of swimming and I didn't know what to think of it: it was part freeing, exhilarating and a bit scary. I moved to the other end where it was not so deep and stayed within that area until it was time to go.

I watched the other girls going up and down, some of them would come out and make repeated jumps over and over again. We finally left after they had had a couple of jumps. By the time, we got home it was almost dark. As we were changing our clothes, my grandmother, whom we simply referred to as Yar or Yah arrived. "You went swimming nor to so."

I giggled. "Yar, did the men finished the work?"

She looked at me blankly and with a light smile she simply nodded. What a relief, I suddenly felt relaxed. My grandmother pointed to the food on the table but I was still full from all that eating in the farm, we had been eating all kind of fruits and vegetables non-stop. I went to the back house to look for Baio and my father, but they were not there. I went to the veranda and everyone was there; it was not as packed as the previous night. Pafinoh was there, my father, Baio and plenty of the cousins. They just sat there, some chatting and some playing. At the front of the house, just across the road, were various small shops, people were selling char Cole grill corns, peanuts, meat skewers, donuts, all sorts of food. It all smelt so good, sometimes I would take repeated deep breaths just to take all the pleasant smells in. I also noticed two tins on the veranda. One was for Yar and the other was for Mami Iye; they were both selling tobacco. It was made up of tobacco leaves which were processed and then ground into a powder form called *snoff*. They then tied it into small bits in plastic bags. People would come to buy the snoff or *thabaca* as it was also called. A lot of elderly men and women consumed thabaca on a regularly basis. We played just outside of the house under the moon shine. We were there until we got tired before we went to bed.

When I woke up in the morning, Yar was getting dressed. She was wearing finely fitted clothes. "Where are you going?" I knew this was not how she dressed for the farm.

"I am going to church, it's a Sunday today," she replied. "Am coming with you." I rushed off to wash my face and get dressed then off we went to the church.

After church we spent the rest of the day doing other work in town. No trip to the farm on that Sunday. Fudia and I watched as my grandmother preboiled the rice, or *panboil* as we called it.

After the preboiled process, the rice was dried under the sun. Yar would come and gently turn it over from time to time. When it had been dried enough, it was time to take the husk out of the rice through the *mortar-odoh* and the mortar and pestle. They used the *fannar* to separate the husk from the rice, then the cleaned grains of rice were stored in the chop box or somewhere else. With all that going on, I noticed my father's younger brother for the first time. He was not as slim and tall as my father, he was medium height, a bit round with plenty of facial hair. As he was approaching, the other children said it was Uncle Albert, and they elbowed each other gently to alert them. He came and everyone suddenly behaved themselves. "Good afternoon uncle," we greeted. He paused briefly, looked around to where we were sitting, and he nodded gently. What was it with my father and his brother, they didn't seem to be saying much. There was something mysterious about them. Everyone tended to behave themselves whenever they were around. The younger students in the school where my father taught would run into their classrooms or just stop talking as he approached; I had seen it on the days we walked to school together. I had heard them call him strict.

By the time we finished taking the husk out of the rice it was evening. The process of beating the rice as it was called was fun and thoroughly tiring. We had dinner and retired early to bed on that day. The next day was another farm day and we had to wake up very early in the morning. I went to bed excited about the prospect of going to the farm. If I was given a choice between staying in town and going to the farm, I would choose to go to the farm with Yar every time.

Second time on the farm was a bit different. Not too far from the swamp was a large patch of land with rice growing on it. They called it *furn furn*, *furn furn*. It was the seed of rice, which was pre-planted. When it reached the preferred height, it was then carefully uprooted and replanted on the swamp. You uprooted it, shook off the mud and tied it up into smaller bundles. If you stored it properly by putting it upright on the roots, it would keep for a long period of time before it died out. We spent the next couple of days uprooting the furn furn and storing it properly. Baio and Uncle joined us from time to time. Father's younger brother Uncle Albert was doing modern agriculture as we called it at that time. He had his own farm. He lived in Fadugu with my grandmother. Instead of having a lot of people digging the soil for him as they did for Yar and others, he had a machine which was somehow hooked or strapped onto two cows; as the cows moved, with someone guarding them, the soil got dug up. It was a faster way to dig the soil. It was only him and a very few other people who had that kind of machinery in the township. His own farm was quite a distance away from his mother, my grandmother, so we hardly saw him.

The farm was calm, there was no big cooking going on like the other days. We just had some vegetables and plenty of fruits which we ate all through the day. Getting the furn furn ready to be replanted was all we did in the next couple of days until the day for the planting. This time it was the women's turn to take on the swamp, they were the ones doing the planting. The singing, playing, joking, disagreements, the cooking, everything happened at the same time and it happened so fast. No explanations would do it justice, you had got to be there to see it, to experience it, to hear it.

We all joined in the planting process, you held the furn furn on one hand and you used the other hand to insert the rice into the swamp. Spending time with my grandmother was one of my happiest childhood memories.

There was not much to do in the farm after the planting was completed. Yar and others only went there from time to time to make sure everything was going on well. Someone had to keep watch every now and again because the cows from the other farmers could come to the farm and eat up all the rice if you did not keep an eye on it. Only one or two people went there regularly to keep the cows and other animals away.

Most of our days were now spent in the town getting to know more family members. It was a very large family. We would meet a family member every day. I got to spend some time with Yanor. My mother had told me stories about how she liked to carry me on her back all day when I was a baby. My mother said she hardly put me down or let anyone else carry me around. Some nights Yanor, Fudia and I would go over the street to buy roast corn, or roast vegetables, or donuts and we would sit on the veranda and eat. We also interacted with my cousins a lot more as the days went on.

One evening after dinner my father told us to get ready as we would be leaving in two days' time. "I thought it's the long holidays. How come we are going back so soon?" I asked my father. He smiled one of his slow smiles and simply said, "There is only one week remaining; we have to get ready because school reopens the following week." A wave of sadness automatically set in. Why did time go by so quickly without even giving us any notification, I thought to myself.

And immediately thought about how Cisi was doing in her new placement. Everyone had been asking after her in Fadugu. The day before we left, Yar was busy packing all kinds of food for us to take. We had come with few pieces of luggage and now we had so many bags to take with us. The day before we left for Magburaka, Yar kept asking me if I was ok, maybe she could see what I was feeling. I really did not want to go back, not so soon anyway, I wished my grandmother was coming with us. She was so warm, and as strong as an ox.

The day came for us to return, we had breakfast in the back of the house. Yar did not came to the front, we did our farewell at the back of the house. I held her closely, then she whispered, "Greet your mama for me." We said our goodbyes to everyone else who was around and boarded a vehicle which had come from Kabala and was heading to Makeni.

Chapter 5

"Who put this roofing zinc under this table?" Crashing sounds! "They should not be here." Another crashing sound! "This is where the children spend most of their time in the evenings." A few moments of silence went by. "If they scratch themselves on this zinc they could get tetanus." More crashing sounds! I got up and slowly walked towards the direction of the sounds and the crash. It was my mother Cisi: she was removing the zinc which someone had placed underneath the table on the veranda. She was throwing them away as she spoke. I just stood there watching her. It was not a dream; the sounds were actually happening. All of a sudden, she screamed on the top of her lungs, dropped the zinc she was holding, then she ran away from the veranda screaming, "SNAKE! SNAKE! SNAKE!"

I ran from the door frame where I was standing, heading towards my mother. "Where is it?" someone asked. She pointed. "It is on the veranda under the last roofing zinc sheets on the floor." Some men rushed to where my mother was pointing. They were holding sticks, one of them flipped the table while another one helped to remove it out from the veranda. The men immediately started striking the zinc and they kept striking it until there were no more movements. Then they stopped and lifted the zinc up.

There it was, a cobra, as one of the men shouted and threw it where a small crowed of us had gathered. It was big, and very long, the men used one of the sticks they had been using to strike the snake to measure it up. The slithering thing laid there motionless and everyone was talking and pointing.

Uncle Brima appeared from nowhere, took the stick from one of the men and started striking the dead snake. He said, "YOU! YOU! YOU!" to the snake and he said it with every strike. He did it with such dramatical effect that everyone just started laughing. Even Cisi, who had barely said a word or moved from where she was standing, smiled. That was Uncle Brima for you, he knew how to defuse intense situations by joking and making everyone laugh, especially making my mother calm down. And it was him, Uncle Brima, who had stored the roofing zinc underneath the table as we later found out. My father asked him to find somewhere else to store it. That was our first day back. Well, hello Magburaka I said to myself.

My mother had come back a few days before we got there. We arrived so late at night we could not even unpack. After the snake fiasco we started unpacking. As we were doing so, Cisi told us that she had been offered a permanent position in Matotoka town. She was going to be the main midwife in and around the surrounding villages. "You will be combining the cooking with Brima," she explained. "It will be fine, Jibrila and Edward will also help." We said nothing, we just listened. I would have been around seven to eight years old by now.

The following day, we all left the house at the same time, all of us walked out of the house and as we reached the front of Pa-abu-Larkoh's house, Cisi bid us farewell and told us she would come back regularly. She went on to say we could come to stay with her during the weekends.

"How are we going to get there?" asked Baio.

"I will make arrangements for a driver to take you there, don't worry, I have already discussed it with one of the drivers." She left and headed towards the car park where she could get transportation for Matotoka. Uncle was just standing there waiting for us. We ran and joined him, then we all proceeded to our own various schools.

When we came back from school on that day, all the uncles were there including my father. They were doing the cooking. My father was marking papers. We changed and went to help out as usual; there was not much left to do except to wash the dishes. As we waited for the rice to finish cooking, I went and sat close to my father, watching as he did the marking of the papers. In some questions he would give one mark, some two marks, some a half mark, when he had finished, he would calculate all the marks the person had scored and total it up. The paper of the individual which he was marking scored 49½ per cent. Just as he was about to enter the marks as a final score, I told him, "Uncle, wait, can you just round it up to 50 per cent?" because 50 per cent was the pass mark, anything below 50 per cent meant you had not passed the paper. "You are not going to fail him for a half mark are you?" He turned towards me, with the hand which was holding the red pen, he slowly put down his glasses, smiling as he said, "Even if it was you, I would still put down the 49½ per cent If that is what you scored that is what I am going to put down." He turned around and entered the 49½ per cent mark. He continued with the next paper. Someone just failed a paper because of a half mark, I shook my head as I thought to myself.

That was just the way my father was. If you came to borrow his axe for chopping wood, you made sure you brought it back when you had finished using it. If he had to go back to your place and pick it up from there, then when you needed it next time, whatever you did, you just didn't come back to him. There was no way he was going to let you use it again. I had heard him say countless times, "If you borrow something, you should carry it or bring it back." Something like that.

The uncles dished up the food and it was time to eat. It was nothing like my mother's cooking or my grandmother's cooking, but at least it was edible. That was the way it was until all the uncles started disappearing one by one. Uncle Brima got a job at Margbass. It was a company which used sugar canes to produce sugar and alcohol called *sas-man* and *afames*. Sas-man was a spirit-like liquid and it just looked clear like water, and afames was the lesser version of sasman and the afames looked a bit like tea with no milk. I knew this because Uncle Brima sometimes brought some with him in smaller containers and he would explain to anyone who was watching, he would tell them the differences. Uncle Brima was working on shifts, some nights and some days. Uncle Edward had a job at the same government hospital where my mother was working and training. Jibrila started training to become a driver. As the time went on it was just my father, Fudia, Baio and I left in the house.

Chapter 6

Before we left school one morning, my father called us and showed us a place where he would be putting some money with a list. He said we could use that list to take with us to the market. He looked at Fudia as he spoke, "After school go to the market and buy this and that." He started calling the names on the list, we nodded and left for school.

When we came back from school, we collected the money and the list then set off to the market. Isatu our friend and neighbour came with us. She showed us the way because she went to the market almost every day to do her elder sister's shopping. She also knew all the short routes to the market. Isatu even had people whom she bought from regularly.

They were called *cos-ter-ment*, which just meant "regular customers". As she guarded us amongst the women, you could not miss the noisiness and fast pace of the women. How they called at you to get you to buy from them, it was all so confusing. Everyone was talking and yelling, and it sounded as though they were doing it together.

We got all the items we needed and left. Uncle had already brought some vegetables from his garden; we set the fire and started the cooking process. For the first time, Fudia was the head cook and I was the assistant head cook. Baio and Uncle were the second-assistant cooks I supposed. Am not going to lie that was the worst cooking I had tasted. We somehow ate it around late in the evening and went to bed.

That lasted for a few weeks and my father stopped coming home after school. He went straight to

Rogbonm again for socialising. We would come home to complete silence in our apartment. It was just the three of us now, we had no one to give us instructions or directions. We had to put everything we had learnt from spending time around the kitchen into good use. Fudia would collect the money from the usual place and go to the market while I stayed at home to start the fire and sometimes started with the boiling of the rice or the chopping and cutting of the vegetables before she got back. It was a long distance from our house in Bangura Street to the market. By the time Fudia returned from the market the sun was not that hot anymore. I went to the kitchen and tried to start the fire. The wood was wet because we had left it outside and it had rained. I collected it, put it on the fire stones, collected some fire coal from the other women's fireplace, I placed it on the wood and started to blow. I blew with my mouth but the wood would not light up. I collected a lead cover and started to blow frantically, by now I was covered with ash which was already on the fireplace.

The ash was on my hair, my face and all over my body yet there was no fire. The wood was completely soaked. After a while I removed all the wood from the fire stones and scattered them all over the kitchen. I then collected a cup of water and poured it all over the fireplace. I sat back with my head on my knees, my hands holding my feet. I was wiping in frustration slowly. I didn't know how long I was seated like that, but I was brought back from my misery with a soft voice and a soft tap on the shoulders, "Mormi what happened, what is the matter?" It was Fudia. I just pointed to the fireplace unable to speak. She said, "Oh, the wood is soaked, you could not start the fire and you poured water all over the fireplace?"

She looked at me with a funny expression and we both started laughing. "Come let's go." she urged me. We left the kitchen and sat in the living room in complete silence. It was already turning dark and still my father had not returned. Fudia put the shopping inside the house. We had not eaten anything since we had breakfast in the morning.

My younger brother's face was exactly how I felt. It was now completely dark and there was nothing we could do. Fudia brought the lamps out and used the match to light them up. Just as we were about to go to bed my father appeared. He took one look at us and just handed us the plastic bag he was holding. There were three loafs of bread and some butter inside, it even contained some cubes of sugar. That was supposed to be our breakfast, but we ended up having it for dinner.

We went to school with no breakfast the next day. My father gave us some coins to buy food during lunch time at school. I was in the classroom but all I could think about was how we were going to be able to cook. When we got home, the hunger in my stomach kept showing up every few minutes as if to remind me that it was still there and still needed sorting out. The other girls in school had always chosen me to play during break time because we would play so many games and it was usually between two groups. But this time I could not play, my head was hurting, it was not only because I was so exhausted from fetching water in the morning, and from blowing the fire for God knows how long, but it was because my uniform had become so short and tight, I didn't want to be jumping around showing my underwear, or because my uniform was so tight, it might just rip on the sides. I sat down and watched them as they played. My mind wanted to join in but the body had no energy. From time to time Uminatu would look over and wave at me to join in. I would simply shake my head and remain seated. Then it occurred to me that our father had given us some coins as lunch money. I went and found Fudia, we then got ourselves some bread and beans. It was called,

cosho en brad.

Uncle was at home when we came back from school. And there was a lot of dry chopped wood from our own side of the kitchen. The shopping was on a tray. I asked if he did the shopping himself. "No, I gave one of the women some money and the list," he told us. "I asked her to do our own shopping when she went to do her hers." He brought out the match, poured some kerosine on the wood and lit up the fire. We finished cooking that day before it got dark. Even though the food was ready, I was still scared to eat because whenever I had not eaten for a long while it would hurt my stomach a lot after I ate. The tiny pangs of pains would last for a long time on the stomach. We ate our food; the rice was cooked well but the plasas not so much. At least we had a lot left over to warm up in the morning and eat before school.

Cisi said she was going to come home on the weekends or we could go to visit her on the weekends but still she had not visited and we had not been to Matotoka yet.

One day we came home from school and one of the women in the compound told us, "Your mother came this morning, just after you left for school, she left you some items, they are on your veranda." She also told us we should just go to the car park and tell the driver that we are the children of nurse Agnes, he would take us to her place at Matotoka. We immediately dashed down to check on what she had left for us. The first thing we all noticed were the sheep tone mangoes. We devoured them in less than no time. I didn't know about the others but my stomach was feeling a bit pleased with itself. Judging by the smiles on their faces I could say the same for them. I had not eaten mangoes like that since I had left Fadugu. There were cassava, potatoes, raw bananas, ripe bananas; they were a pleasant surprise to come home to after school.

Chapter 7

Our cooking had improved immensely, we simply stayed away from cooking the difficult dishes (plasas) We now knew what we could cook and what we could not cook. We stayed away from cooking cassava leaves, *krain-krain* and all of the other leafy green vegetables that took too long to cook. We opted for the less time-consuming cooking plasas, such as soups and pepper. They were quicker and more edible to eat.

One Friday we told Uncle we were going to visit Cisi in Matotoka after school. He simply nodded and asked how we were going to get there. We explained, and he told us to be careful. From school we went straight to the car park. The driver was there, it was a Peugeot taxi, we told the driver what our mother had said, and he said, "You came late, the car is already full, I have taken money from all of these passengers and cannot turn them back; it was the last trip of the day." Deflated was an understatement. Just as we turned away and started walking back, he called after us.

One of the women had offered to let my younger brother sit on her lap and there was not much luggage in the boot of the car. "You two can manage in the boot if you really want to see your mother." I was hesitant, I looked to Fudia for reassurance, but she was already climbing and finding ways to make herself comfortable.

That was one of things I admired about Fudia. She always knew when I needed her reassurance, which was why she would give it to me by doing it herself, usually without saying a word. We squeezed ourselves in to the boot of the car like cargo. It was about an eight to ten-mile trip, may be less, maybe more, and the road was good, straightforward, flat and tar. No hills, no bumps, or too many potholes. "We will arrive in no time don't worry." the driver reassured us as he closed the door of the boot where we sat. We looked at each other, not knowing what to say. I watched the trees on the side of the road as the car drove by. That was all I could remember until I was woken up by Fudia when everyone was getting off the Peugeot. When I got down, I could not turn my neck to the other side, my body felt stiff and we were sweating. We asked the driver where the clinic or hospital was, and he said, "Get in the car, am going home now, I will drop you there, your mother is my neighbour and I have to collect the fare for the three of you anyway." This time the three of us sat together inside the car and it was only the three of us in the whole car.

He dropped us right at the hospital, and handed us over to our mother. The crowd was just starting to disperse when the driver walked in and we followed closely. My mother was sat on a chair and she had placed her hands on a large table in front of her. She was wearing a light pink uniform dress, and white apron at the front of the uniform, the uniform also had a large white floppy colour on the neck. She had some round white thing sitting on top of her head which was part of the uniform. They quickly exchanged a few words and she opened a drawer from the table and gave him some money, he turned to us, waved and he was gone. We greeted the people around and some of them asked questions about us, I heard a woman saying, "Na you pekin them?" to which she replied, "Yes, they are my children."

"Then feber you, the boy pekin more," the woman went on to say. We sat on one of the benches by the side until she had finished dealing with all of the hospital patients.

Eventually we got to my mother's new home; it was a large house with a huge backyard space in the front and in the back. Most of the houses were similar to each other in that street or road.

My mother introduced us to the landlady, she was an elderly woman about the same age as my grandmother. Her name was Ya-mariama fulla. Ya-mariama fulla was looking after one of her daughter's children: Alie, Amadu, Haja, and Pohsai. There were also other relatives' children, Momodu and Rita, plus a few grown-ups. The grandchildren were about our age, we were older than some and some were older than us. After the greetings, the washing and the eating, my mother left us and went out. Rita and Lamrana were really friendly, they kept asking us questions and comparing notes, for instance Lamrana asked me what kind of milk did I prefer in my tea. "Is it the powdered milk or liquid peak milk?"

"Peak milk," I answered.

"That is the one I like too," she replied.

I didn't know if that was entirely true, because sometimes when I was asked to go and bring the powdered milk, I would quickly open it and scoop a few spoons into my mouth. By the time I arrived to where I was supposed to take it, it would have dissolved in my mouth then I would wipe my mouth so the traces could not be found. But my mother could always tell if I had done that, she would look at me then look at the tin of milk, then she would either shake her head or give me the look which said I know you've had a few scoops. It was probably the powdered milk because you could keep it for longer than the liquid milk. She went on to tell me she did not like sardines but she liked luncheon meat. I nodded.

Most of this food she was naming I was aware of, but I only ate them occasionally. It looked like she ate them regularly. Lamrana also told me her mother and father lived in Koidu town in Kono. She said her father was a diamond digger who had about five or seven wives. They all lived in the same house, but every wife had their own place.

I thought about my father only having one wife. Look at the drama between them, with all those wives only God knows what their everyday life would be like. Was that why they were staying with their grandmother? Rita called out for both of us, "Come on you two we are ready, let's play cou cou." The moon was shining on full bloom. Cou cou was more like hide and seek, plus tig all rolled into one. When they said go, everyone would find a place to hide while one person would go searching. If they found you and touched you, then it was your turn to do the chasing or the finding. We kept on playing, taking turns to chase, run and hide until it was bedtime when Ya-mariama fulla called out then it was time for everyone to go to bed. As they did, we went to bed too.

One good thing about my mother, she always made sure there was enough food in the house. In Matotoka there was plenty of cooking oil, milk, vegetables, different varieties of rice, meat, fish, lots of live chicken and eggs. Women from the nearby villages would bring all sorts of livestock or food stuff for my mother. It was either as a thank you or as payments if they didn't have the physical cash to pay for their treatments. When she made breakfast and left for work in the morning, we knew exactly what to do. We cooked *foo-foo* and *granat* soup for lunch. We even took some for her at the clinic. She was not expecting it. "Did you cook this?" We both nodded somehow feeling proud of our expedition. She ate a little bit of it and said it was really good, it just needed more salt.

Fudia was the boss for turning foo-foo, her foo-foo always came out clear with no lumps and it was always hard. She did not like her foo-foo to be soft. We returned back to the house. By midday my mother had someone drop us off some cooking items. "Your mother has been called to a nearby village about two to three miles away to check on a pregnant woman. Cook and eat dinner she might be running late." The woman said her goodbyes then she left us to it. No problem, like I said there was dry wood and everything we needed for cooking, it was not as difficult as cooking in Magburaka. We took out the pots and pans and started cooking. Just as Fudia was putting the rice down from the fire we heard the sound of a motorcycle, and all of a sudden, most of the children around the area were shouting "KDK" and he revved the engine of his motorcycle, sounded the horn loudly and he responded "Kankar-ardikor!" The children shouted again the same thing, "KDK" and he repeated the same thing, "Kankan-ardikor!" They repeated the back and forth between them a few times. It was a bit entertaining somehow.

The engine stopped and both of them got off the motorcycle. Once the greetings were over with Mr KDK, as he was commonly called, Cisi dished up the food and we ate. Rice was our staple food in my place, it was eaten on a regular basis. An individual could eat all kinds of food or snacks, if they had not eaten a meal of rice, they would still say, "I have not eaten all day." That was how important eating rice at least once a day was.

The weekend came and went just like that. We were supposed to return to Magburaka on Sunday, but our hair had not been braided. The person who was to braid it was nowhere to be found. When Cisi came back late that evening and saw that our hair was undone she was not happy. She sat us down and did it herself. Let's just say my mother doing hair was not something I would recommend to anyone. I thought now that she had her own place of work, we would see her a lot more. There were no significant changes anyway. She left in the morning for work and returned late in the evening yelling and snapping at everything and everyone. Especially with me, and Fudia, she criticised everything. She would say things like a woman is not supposed to sit like that, don't talk like that, or chew your food in that manner, don't speak with your mouth full, don't answer me back or talk when am talking it is disrespectful, don't walk like that, your legs are too long, look at your eyes, put your eyes down, don't look me in the eyes when am talking. Et cetera, et cetera, those were just a few of the everyday points of corrections we had to go through.

It came to the point where I was more at ease when she was not around. One day, after one of her critic sessions, Aunty Baby, her younger sister, said to me, "Don't mind her it's not your fault you look just like your father, as soon as she sees you, she sees your father hence the sudden little outburst."

By Monday afternoon we were back in Magburaka; Uncle was not happy because we had missed a day in school.

We brought back a lot of food and pocket money to last us for the week, we used it to buy food at lunchtime in school. There were no school dinners, you either took your own food to eat during break time, bought food at lunch time, or just watched everyone else eat, or found a way to distract yourself and the hunger in your stomach. Whenever we left my mother, it would be another couple of days, sometimes weeks, before we could see her again.

My mother hardly came to stay with us in Magburaka anymore, it was now up to us to find ways to go back and forth between both parents: the parents who put their careers and social lives first. We loved staying in Matotoka despite her temper tantrums; the house was always full with people, you could never come home to an empty house like we did in Magburaka. The children of Mr KDK were now staying with my mother, all three of them: two boys and a girl. The two boys were both called John and the girl was called Mormi as well, because there were now two Mormis in the house, there was Mormi big and Mormi small. Combined with the grandchildren and the landlady it was a very full house. There was never a dull moment. We wanted to be in Matotoka every weekend. I even asked my mother if we could go to school with Mr KDK's children in Matotoka. She explained to me how she had already discussed that with my father. It was not a positive outcome for her or for us because my father insisted we stayed with him, and we stayed in school in Magburaka with no further discussions. Sometimes it would be even months before we could go to my mother's place due to transportations. We started to discuss these issues of not being with our mother amongst ourselves, and we started looking for how we could get there.

The driver who had been taking us was no longer around. One day we went to the car park, entered one of the cars and sat comfortably: it was a bigger car with more passenger seats. Since the transport fare was usually collected at the end of the journey, it was fine by us. When we arrived, the driver asked us for the transport fare, we started rummaging in our bags looking for money that was not there. As soon as the driver turned around to collect the fare from another passenger Fudia looked at us and with a nod she took off running.

Baio and me took off after her. We ran as fast as we could, we already knew all the bypass routes to the house. I could hear the driver shouting, "I know your mother the nurse, am going to ask her for my money." We knew he could not leave the other passengers to come after us, but what if he did come after us. I asked Fudia and she said he could not do so. "Why would he risk leaving the other passengers when he was still collecting their fares?" I must tell you that was thrilling and so very scary. After we reached a safe place, I was laughing and shaking, our little plan worked out on this occasion. We did not say anything to my mother, she found out from the driver.

We did not have the guts to go to that car park and face the driver again. On another occasion we decided to walk the whole journey after school. We decided to not waste time on Friday after school, we would not go back to house. It would be time-consuming. The assumption was because it was not that far by car it would not be too far on foot. It was one of those very hot sunny days; the sun was hotter than usual in the dry season. We decided amongst the three of us to walk the whole journey all by ourselves. We had not even made a quarter of the journey, we could barely speak, we were thirsty and our feet were starting to feel blistery in the flip-flops under the heat, we had no water with us. Baio and Fudia were in front of me and they suggested we should take a break, there was a small tree which gave small shade, there were also small bushes by the wall of the road. Both of them were leaning on the wall when, as I approached to join them, I saw a brown snake very slowly coming towards Baio and I screamed my brother's name with all the strength I had left. He moved in a panic and the snake missed him just by the neck. The three of us just stood there speechless watching the snake crawl away. We did not stop again except when we asked for water from a nearby village.

It was so dark by then we could not see the road properly, we had to hold on to one another for comfort and courage. Why did we risk walking, and why was the distance more than double all of a sudden? It was really a long distance to walk I thought to myself. Luckily the moon started to shine and it was not that dark anymore, and we were not as scared as we were before the moon came out.

My mother was not expecting us and she was completely shocked and fearful by our arriving so late at night.

We told Cisi about how we walked the whole journey and about the snake and she said firmly we should never risk our lives or put ourselves in danger like that again.

When we got back to Magburaka, I noticed this woman coming to visit Uncle Brima in the evenings, sometimes she would bring her daughter with her. The visits became regular as the time went on. We would all sometimes join in the story times or just sit around and listen to them.

Chapter 8

Uncle Brima got married to Cici Fatu. His wife was tall, round and beautiful. She had a child from a previous marriage. She brought her daughter and her younger sister when she came to live with Uncle Brima. That reduced the workload on us for a bit. Uncle, my father, and Uncle Brima decided that Cici Fatu could now do all the cooking while we went back to our original role of fetching water, beating pepper, sometimes fetching wood, washing the dishes and washing our clothes. She cooked really well, but the food she put in the bowl for her younger sister and the three of us to eat seemed really small.

Her sister was way older than us, she ate really fast; because we ate with our hands, the food could burn your hands if you were not careful. Could her sister not feel how hot the food was, I thought as we ate. She would finish all the food in front of her side of the bowl and then carry on eating the food in front of us. The three of us were used to eating at our own pace now. I thought we would have to up our eating game or we would never be able to keep up with her.

It was still a relief to not have to worry about going to the market and starting a fire every day. Some days we would came home and Cici Fatu was already cooking. Her younger sister would do all the necessary helping or supporting in the kitchen sometimes. Therefore, we now had time to play with the other children. It was play time with Isatu and Pa-wusu or we could just do our homework.

One day we followed Pa-wusu and Isatu to pick some oranges from the house next door; just between the back of our compound house and the other houses was a huge orange tree. Pa-wusu, Isatu and I climbed up the tree, we had a way to tie the clothes we were wearing tightly. Any orange we picked was put into the inside of our backs. Our clothes acted as a sack to hold the oranges. We would drop the oranges for Baio and Fudia to collect after we had had our sacks stuffed. Having the tie or knot secured was paramount. We had been in situations in which the tie became loose and all the oranges could drop from your back. The biggest issue with that was that the drop or sounds could alert the owners or elders and land you with some serious punishment. We were busy rummaging for oranges on top of the dark tree when one of the residents pointed a torch light towards the tree. Isatu whispered, "Don't move, every one stay still." It was only at that very moment I started to feel the movements of tiny things crawling all over my body.

I knew what they were because I was familiar with the bites of the red ants, especially from that tree, they were always present on it, and on this day, they were biting me all over my body. I could have wet myself from the fear of getting caught and from the biting of the red ants. The torch light lingered a bit and then it went off. As soon as the flashlight was off, we quickly and slowly got down from the tree. Then we slowly on tippy toes left the area. Fudia and Baio had already walked away from where they had been standing. We only managed to get a few oranges due to the interruption of the torch light or flashlight.

When I woke up in the morning, there were bruises and tiny bite marks all over my body. The bite marks I could have argued that I didn't know how I had got them: it must have been the mosquito's bite or any other insects. But the bruising was not something to easily fob off. Now I had to hide the bruising from my father. If he saw them, he would want to know how I got them. There must be an explanation. Then I would have to face the consequences for going out late at night and for climbing the tress.

And for doing so without permission from the owner. Some days we would go raiding a corn farm or garden at night. As long as it was not raining and the moon was shining, we would go in search of fruits or vegetables. Where there was hunger there was nothing off limits within our surroundings.

In the morning or during the day when we would go to fetch water, that was when we would high mark the corn which was ready or almost ready for harvest. And at night we would go and get it, we used our hands to get a feel of the corn inside. You would be able to tell just by touching it. Other days it would be our own father's garden which he used to teach his agricultural practical. We would dig up all the sweet potatoes, boil them and eat them. Other days we would cut off some of the sugar cane in his garden and have a chew on them. How could I forget the pawpaw it was our little treat most days after school. The pawpaw tree was the most challenging one to climb for me. It had no branches. Fudia and Baio would somehow make themselves into a human climbing ladder, they would give me a shoving start until I had wrapped my hands and feet on the pawpaw tree. Then I was on my own. I would use my feet to hold on while I dragged my upper body upward. I had no idea how I would get on top of that tree but I did. I would pick the ripe ones or the ones that were almost ripe. Coming down the pawpaw tree was more painful than getting on it. It was just a zooming fall, holding onto the tree, brushing and bruising your chest all the way down. I had to somehow control my body not to hit the ground with too much impact or force.

After school we sometimes removed the seeds inside and ate them. Or Fudia would make our favourite; she would peel the pawpaw, cut it into medium chunks, sprinkle some cayenne pepper, add some jumbo maggi and a squeeze of lime juice. Give that a little shake and you had yourself a delicacy. It tasted really good, the sweetness from the pawpaw, the tanginess from the lime and the heat from the pepper all worked together to give you an unusual but unique good taste. For me at least, it was one of my favourite things to eat after school before we cooked our own dinner.

My father did not come home from school anymore, we either saw him in the mornings, weekends or when he woke us up late at night so we could open the door for him. Sometimes we would mistakenly lock the door from inside when we went to bed. And sometimes it was not a mistake, we just got scared and put the bolt on. One time I think he must have been standing outside for a very long time waiting for us to open the door, we must have been sleeping really deeply and did not hear his knocking. Eventually, as soon as I opened the door, I was greeted with a couple of lashes all over my body. It was not even me who had locked the door, I just happened to be the one who opened it I thought as I rubbed where he had whipped me.

There was no need to go to Matotoka every weekend now. All we had to worry about now was how to get our hair braided for school, unbraided hair or hair extensions were not allowed in our school. Getting my hair braided was a bit of a big deal because it was longer and thicker than most of the other girls, and when I washed it, it got tangled up and became painful to comb or braid. So, we had to do chores or errands or just be really respectful towards the ones who did our hair, that was our payment for braiding.

One Saturday morning Uncle woke up early and we asked him if we could go with Mabinty the younger sister of Cici Fatu to the river to wash our clothes; we had tried going with Isatu and Pa-wusu before but my father had said no, he said it was too dangerous for us, we needed an adult to go with us. Mabinty was more or less an adult. He agreed but warned us not to swim in the river. We packed all our dirty clothes and uniforms with soap bars and left. I had always wanted to go to the Pampamna river on Saturdays like everyone else. The ones who usually went to the river came back with happy faces and all sorts of stories. But my father had always forbidden us from doing so. Instead, we would fetch water all day to wash our clothes at home. It was a joy when he agreed for us to go. The five of us left the compound, we had finally got to go with Isatu and Pa-wusu and Mabinty. When we arrived, I was fascinated, the river was not only ten time bigger, wider and faster than the one in Fadugu but it was packed with people: people around my age. The school where my father taught, the boys school was a boarding school and must of them were there too. I even saw people from my own school, so this was why everyone wanted to come to the Pampamna river on a Saturday. It was buzzing, some were doing their laundries and others were swimming, some were sitting on the rocks or just standing around. We quickly finished our laundry, put it aside then joined the swimming. Even though Uncle had warned us not to swim, we did anyway.

Thank goodness I had learnt how to hold my breath and stay afloat in Fadugu. We kept going under the water and we would swim all the way to the middle in the deeper end and then return back to the shallow end. We repeated it until we got tired, caught our breaths and then went in again. One time I dived down and when I lifted my head up in the middle of the river I came face to face with a snake, a black shiny snake; it was similar to the one that was killed on our veranda. I froze, I was not expecting a snake to be in the water, I thought snakes could only be on dry land. I had no idea these scary wiggling things could swim too. It was staring at me; all I could do was stare back with everything inside of me quaking. For a few seconds I thought this was it, it was going to bite me, who was going to save me, my mother was not around to cut out wherever the bite was, and then put something that looked like a stone, which sucked and removed all the poison out. I had watched her do it a few times. And if I died on that day, my father would have said, "Didn't I warn you not to swim."

Then the snake just turned away, gladded on top of the water holding its head above the water. The black reflection from its skin gave a silvery reflection on the water as it went. I stood there feeling numb watching it until it disappeared. I dared not go in the middle of the river again yet we continued swimming until it was late in the afternoon. When we got back my father took one look at us and spoke,

"You have been swimming, haven't you?" We said nothing, how did he know we had been swimming, was it because our eyes had become as red as the sunset or was it the smiles and enthusiasm that had exposed us?

There was not much to do at school because it was the end of another school year. It was time for the six-week holidays. We decided to spend it at Matotoka.

This time Uncle took us to the car park and paid our fares himself; the story of walking to Matotoka and the snake almost biting Baio in the neck must have frightened him. It frightened all of us for a very long time and sometimes when he annoyed me, I would just say, "I should have left that snake to bite you." And my mother would say, "Please don't ever say that again."

At Matotoka, everything was still the same. Except, the mother of Amadu, Lamrana, Alie and Poshea came to stay with her children for a couple of days. She also planned on taking her children with her so they could spend the holidays with their father in Kono. Amadu's mother and my mother had become good friends over the years. She kept on saying to me, "I think my son Amadu likes you." She would look at her son smiling and laughing. Sometimes she would say, "You are going to be Amadu's wife one day." Even his grandmother and sisters kept saying things like that. I didn't know what brought that idea on because Amadu and I had never even said a word to each other, he was always grumpy and always frowning. If his grandmother asked him to go and help Momudu to look after the sheep or to go help out in the farm, he would refuse.

His response was, am here to go to school not to do all this other work and he would disappear.

The only time I ever got close to Amadu was when we played coucou under the moon shine; he would somehow always find a way to stand near me. Coucou was like a game of hide and seek with tig all rolled into one. One person would shout coucou, then the rest had to find a hiding place. When the person who was seeking found you and tapped you, it would be your turn to do the finding, the chasing and the tapping. Amadu would have been around ten or eleven years old at that time, maybe a year or so older than I was. The next few days they all left for Koidu town. Rita and Momodu did not go with them, the house felt empty all of a sudden.

But we were quick to discover that my mother had opened a pub of her own, like a rum bar. This was where she disappeared to after she finished work from the clinic. The bar was situated on the Kono Road. Passengers would stop over to have drinks and pepper soup from the bar. Her younger sister would help to run the bar while my mother was in the clinic. The bar was packed in the evenings, we would go there in the evenings and spend time in the bar, especially when we knew my mother would return from the clinic and go to the bar thereafter. There was not much for us to do in and around the bar, most times, we would just eat, drink some of the pepper soup, or pass a cup or spoon to an individual.

The bar was always buzzing with all kinds of people. One day my mother brought a magician to perform in the evenings. It was the first time we experienced anything like that. He brought out a razor blade from his mouth, he brought out money from a *tutic*, or plastic bottle, he turned one thing to another thing. He did some tricks and a lot of clothing came out: they were piles of cottons, all brand new. Till this day, I can't comprehend how he did magic, or if they were factual tricks or just pure magic, because when everything was going on, it was impossible for an individual to take their eyes off him or even blink. Our stays at Matotoka were like a flash and a flicker of light at the same time. They came and went before we even processed the facts that we were there.

It was time to start the new week and time to go back to school. When we returned back to Magburaka after the long holiday, I noticed my father was not going out with his friends anymore. He now spent a lot of his time at home. Immediately, my observing antennas came out, they told me something was amiss, but it was difficult to know exactly what it was.

He was not just at home or in his garden planting or uprooting stuff, he was calm and he was saying less each day. Due to this new change in my father, we had to stay inside our living room and study or do homework. Fudia and me did not do well in our school report card that year. Not having time to study before the exams and all that living between Magburaka and Matotoka must have played it part. We passed but only on the borderline. Baio, on the other hand, took first place in class and in almost every subject. When it came to my little brother and his school activities, I don't know how to describe it. He went all in; he took his grades too seriously. If he did not pass a particular subject with a particular percentage, there would be drama or waterworks. He had read big books in front of all the uncles and aunties when he was so small, around the age of four or five years.

That always made him extra happy when Uncle Edward would give him praise or tap his head. Because of the state of our report card, my father decided to give us extra lessons in the evenings. All I could remember from him giving us or giving me extra lessons was a round of lashing. Every time I missed a spelling, there would be whipping.

"Spell about."

"A, A ABUT." Lash on the hand.

"Spell it again."

"A B O U T, about." I repeated loudly shaking my hand to make the sting go away. The man really liked the flogging process or the flogging of people. I would never forget how to spell "about" again. Even when I am in my dying bed if you ask me to spell "about", it will be done.

Chapter 9

Seldomly, my mother would come to see us. She would visit us whenever she was going to Makeni or when she came to Magburaka to get medicine supplies or something. She would come to the house to check on us. Some days she would spend the night and return back the following day and some days it would just be a brief hello and she was gone. It was on one of those visits that it became clear to me the reasons why father was spending time at home. He was having problems with his health.

This discovery was made when Cisi said to him, "The doctor has told you to stop smoking and drinking yet you are still smoking. Do you want to die?" My father said nothing. Smoking? That was news to me, how did she even know my father had smoked that morning? I didn't even know he was a smoker, he had never smoked in front of us or maybe I just could not remember him smoking. But after she said that something hit me, I didn't know what it was but everything felt strange suddenly. Another school year ended, and we were in Matotoka again.

It was a full house as usual. Lamrana had some information for me. She explained that when they went to Koidu town this time, they might not be coming back because after the holiday they might be going to another school. Their mother came and took them away after a few days. Those few days before they left was the first time I saw Amadu relaxed and not grumpy. Maybe he just wanted to be with his mother and father all of the time, I thought to myself. I watched them climb into the car, I watched until the car vanished. Our visits were not the same without them, it was never the same in Matotoka again.

We got back to Magburaka after the holidays. My father's health had still not improved as anticipated. In fact, it was the opposite; it looked like his health was deteriorating.

One day he gave us a note to take to the principal, Mr M M Kamara, explaining that he was taking some time off from teaching. After the principal read the note, he had a worried face, or a worried look. My father was never late for school whatever time he came home, let alone did he take days off. After resting at home, he got his strength back and was back at work. Things seemingly went on in the usual routine. One morning, on the last round of fetching water, Baio was kneeling beside Wonders, the dog, on the veranda. He was crying and calling its name as he shook Wonders gently. "Wonders! Wonders! Wonders! Wake up."

The two of us rushed over to see what was going on. "Why is Wonders not waking up?" Baio simply said to us as he pointed at the non-moving Wonders on the floor. We called for Uncle and he came and took a look at Wonders. Uncle started rubbing my brother's head in a consoling manner. He took a deep breath and with that he said, "Wonders is dead." We were really taken aback because it looked totally fine and healthy. It was not sick or anything of the sort.

My father said to us that the dog was more than eight years old and eight years was a lot of years in a dog's life. He said it must have died from natural causes due to its age. That hit us hard especially Baio who spent most of his time with Wonders. Wonders and Neptune had always been in our family. There was not a time when they were not around. My father must have gotten them when we were little. Wonders was a big male dog with brown colour, and Neptune was a female dog with sand-like colour. My father's favourite line was, "Wonders shall never end", or to any little thing he would say "wonderful"; no wonder he named our dog Wonders.

His health continued to worsen slowly as the time went on. My father must have sent a word of message, or a letter to his mother because one day Uncle Sali came from Fadugu to take him. He said they wanted to go and try some traditional medicines. He also said it would be best for him to be in Fadugu where other family members could help to look after him. But my father did not go with him. He was waiting for the half-term break; more so because he was waiting on his salary to be paid before he could go. It had been over three or four months and the government had not paid the teachers yet. This situation with not getting paid for months was not something new.

We left for Fadudu just a few days after the half-term break. As they welcomed us it was evident that things were not the same anymore. The jumping and playful welcome from the last visit was no more. It was replaced with apprehension, or a calm hello.

Uncle and Baio were taken to their own place and we stayed with our grandmother. It was a different season and a different climate condition. It was not the planting season anymore, it was almost the dry season, just like summer.

The rice and produce which the farmers had planted was about to get harvested. It was the time when the children my age had to really play their own part. They would rise up very early in the morning and go to the farm to chase the birds away. If not, the birds would eat up most of the rice before it was harvested. The grown-ups would build scarecrows and place them all around the farm.

The scarecrows were placed in strategic areas within the rice farm. The boys would also use a catapult which was also called a rubber-fack. They would attach a small stone on it and aim at the birds. The process was commonly called *dreb-bord*. Our visit to Fadudu was supposed to be for a few weeks but we ended up spending the rest of the school year there. We could not go back to Magburaka or go back to school. My father would get better for a few days or a few weeks and then get worse the other week or weeks.

I had not seen my mother for months; we were seated on the veranda one evening when someone shouted, "Cici Agnes." The house was located at the centre of the town; from my grandfather's house in Fadugu, you could see the market, shops and the car park. When someone was coming off a car it was easy for them to be recognised. When I heard her name, I quickly looked over and it was my mother.

I followed the other children and adults who were already running towards her. The following day she told us she had been transferred to a new station, she was going to leave Matotoka and go to Kolifaka. She further explained that she had found a place for us to go and stay while she worked in Kolifaka. "Am still waiting for confirmation," she explained, "the place has links or ways to access medical facilities, you can go to school there and your father can still continue teaching." It all sounded good to me; I was particularly glad about the prospect of going back to school. It was evident that we were going to be apart again and that was something most children would not do a song and dance for. She spent a few days and left. By now I was speaking the Limba language, I was doing almost everything the children my age were doing at that time. Every chore was done every day. I had learnt how to process palm oil from scratch. I was not only harvesting rice, I learnt how to process it, to pre-boil it, and to remove the husk from the rice. I learnt different activities almost every day.

Chapter 10

Schools had re-opened, everyone was going back to school except for the three of us. Just when I was about to give up every hope about ever going to school again, I heard my mother's voice one night. Everyone jumped up shouting, "Na Cisi Agnes." It was almost Christmas. The weather had changed again, it was cold and frosty when we woke up in the morning. Yep, in Africa, some parts get cold and frosty too.

When I got up very early in the mornings to follow the other children to go and dreb-bord, or to chase the birds away, the frost was visible on the leaves, and the mountains were covered with dew; on those mornings it was difficult to see a few metres in front of you.

Then the sun would come out and quickly defrost everything. In the farm, my second cousins, Niyo and Nayomi would go and get wild mushrooms in the bushes. The place looked like an undergrowth, they would also get wild yam. The yam was called *N'dambakin* or something close to what I can remember. They would use nut oil, called *malankor* to fry the mushrooms and the yam was simply boiled. Well come to think of it now, there was nothing more organic than that and the taste stayed with me for a very long time.

We would usually return to town in the evenings, at that point the birds would have stopped coming to eat the rice. When my mother came to collect us, she brought a lot of dresses for everyone, but she did not bring mine, she forgot to pack it, she said. This was only a few days before Christmas. On Christmas Day, most children would have, or expect to have a new set of clothes for that day. It was like a tradition. Not having a new dress, or Christmas-klos as it was called, did not bother me for too long.

All I wanted was for my father to get better and for me to go back to school. Besides, I was selling patch gra-nat in front of the house at nights. Some days I would make gra-nat cake and sell it at the sites of construction workers, or some days it would be oranges, or consho-en-brad. Consho was *gungo* peas and *brad* was bread. We would go in groups to sell. My little aunty, the last daughter of my grandfather, was just a little older than me, Aunty Saryo, she liked to sell different items and I would always go with her. It was her who took me to buy oranges the first time. It was in a village nearby. We arrived in the village with empty rice bags in our hands. She spoke to an elderly man and we gave him some money. The man pointed out the orange trees to us. They were all within reach and some of the oranges could almost touch the ground. There was no need to climb the trees. The oranges were ripe, big and sweet. We carried those oranges on our heads all the way back. In the evening we used a special knife, a small and sharp knife, made only to peel oranges.

The oranges were peeled in a certain way, placed on a tray and sold to passers-by. Some days it would be butterscotch which I would make and sell. Every time I finished selling whatever it was that I was selling I would give the money to my grandmother for safekeeping or I would lose it. I was known for losing things. My father would say, "You are too absent minded," whenever I lost stuff. There was a tailor in town who sold clothes, they were called *tailar made klos*. He sewed them and put them on a hanger around his shop: different styles and different colours. Since my Christmas-Klos was missing in action, or nowhere according to my mother I collected some of the money from my grandmother, then went and bought myself a brand new Christmas-Klos which I wore to church on Christmas morning. After Christmas had past, Cisi came to pick us up. My father's health looked like it was slowly, sort of improving.

We departed and left our father in Fadugu. My father asked my mother where she was taking us and she said she was taking us to a town called Bumbuna. It was the town where the biggest hydroelectricity dam in Sierra Leone was being constructed. The aim of the hydro was to supply the whole county with electricity. "There are regular visits from Bumbuna to Lunsar in case you need to go to the hospital," my mother explained. "Bumbuna also has a secondary school for you to work. You should come there so you can be close with the children," she told my father. He just watched her and said nothing.

We spent the whole day travelling and arrived in Bumbuna very late at night. Cisi took us to her friend's house who was the nurse for Bumbuna town, she was also the wife of the Paramount Chief. Her name was Tha-Nancy. We slept in her house. As I lay in bed, I had all types of questions going through my mind. Are we going to be safe, what if I wanted to run away, where would I go? At least in Magburaka we knew how to get to Matotoka, in Magburaka we had all the uncles and aunties, even though they were hardly around but at least they were there sometimes.

But here, I didn't know anyone, didn't know anywhere and didn't even know where my mother's new station was. Even if I did, I didn't know how to get there. And I said to my mother, or the words came out, "Why can't you just find a place where you can be with us?" I was thinking in my head but the question must have slipped out.

My mother got defensive and she went on the offensive, she started yelling at me, telling me if I only knew what she had to get through to get us a space, she said I was being rude. She even gave me a quick beating on the back as I was lying down. Look, having a beating by an adult member of the family was part of our growing up. It was part of our culture and I received plenty when growing up.

Maybe I shouldn't have been an inquisitive child. I cried myself to sleep. In the morning I thought it was just going to be the three of us going where she was taking us, but she brought out the other children she was already looking after: Lamin, her last sister's son; small Albert, my father's cousin's son; Kali, a boy she was looking after from her new place of work, and someone else; I can see his face now but I just can't remember his name.

We went to a church service that morning and after the service we finally went to meet the head of the place we were going to stay. His name was Father Berton, he was an Italian Roman Catholic priest. He had a place called Mission House. It was run by Italian priests, some nuns, local priests and priests from around West Africa. For example, we had some priests and nuns from Nigeria and Ghana. "Come in, everyone come in and sit down." He shook our hands one by one, as he introduced himself. "Am Father Berton." He said everything in the Krio language, which was a bit unexpected. He was expecting us and already knew all of our names, that was also another surprise. He would call your name and shake your hands. He told us not to worry as there were so many other children of all ages in the mission. He said there were a lot of activities going on every day, we would not get bored. "Come, I will take you so you can have a look around." From the church to the place was not far by car. The mission was located away from the town. There were not many houses around, there were just bushes, or gardens, or farms, where the nuns or sisters lived, which was just a stone's throw away from us. The general overseer, an indigen Mr Cohsi, lived on the other side of our building.

Our building was in the middle of the three structures. The matron Miss Kargbo lived in the mission with us. Father Berton introduced us to Miss Kargbo and some of the girls who were around came to welcome and greet us. He took us to our room or dormitory; it was a long open space with spring beds and spring mattresses on either side of the room. It was the same in the other room: one for the big girls who were in secondary school and one for us who were in primary school. It was all girls; we took a bed each. Fudia shared with small Albert and I shared with Lamin. Albert and Lamin had to stay with us because they were not old enough to live with the boys. Baio and the other two boys were taken to the boys' place.

I felt disorientated, I was grateful to be going back to school but I didn't know this place, I didn't know if I liked it, I didn't know if I wanted to stay there, and I had no idea who these individuals were. The only thing I knew was I had no choice in the situation. Having no choice was the only certainty for us in the whole matter. What if I never saw my father, mother, or grandmother again? Those were the questions consuming me.

After Father Berton who everyone simply called "father" left Miss Kargbo explained the rules to us. The first and most important task of the day was to be in church first thing in the morning. We all had to wake up very early in the morning, wash and go to church for the morning service or morning mass. "Everyone must be in church and on time; I will be in trouble with father, if he does not see you in church," she explained. After church, everyone had to return back to the mission, put on their uniform, eat breakfast and go to school. It was a long walk from the church to the mission, which was situated around the centre of the town. The school was close to where we lived. After school, there was always something to do. We would work in the gardens, sweep the compound, wash our clothes or wash Miss Kargbo's clothes, then cook and eat dinner, before it was time to go back to church for the evening prayer or the rosery. After the rosery, we could play music or some games before we went to bed. It was a very routine structure for every day.

The cooking was done in turns, every one of us had a day in which they did all the food shopping at the marketplace and all the cooking and all the cleaning thereafter. I quickly got on with the girls my age especially the two Mabintys, but I found myself to always be in the company of the older girls. TK or Ramatu were a few of the older girls I quickly became very close to. TK always made me laugh so hard and it was constant. The way she talked, the way she pronounced her words, how she emphasised with the hand gestures, they were all really dramatic. Tigidankay was her full name but everyone just called her TK. It was the same with her elder sister Dormani. We walked to church together and would come back together.

Fudia had also become close with other girls but the two of us remained very close and confided in each other. We would have our little chats to ourselves. TK was like a friend and guardian of some sort. She called me her daughter and I called her my mummy. In the first few weeks I struggled a bit with all the rushing around and having to look after Lamin. But as the days want on, we just got on with it. TK and I are still in contact through Facebook, once in a while, we will talk on the phone. She still calls me her daughter and I still call her my mummy.

Chapter 11

"How come Cisi is not back yet?" I asked Fudia. "Since we separated on the day, we met Father Berton, she has not come back to see us." We were having a discussion when we were having a wash at the back of the house.

"Don't worry about it, you know Cisi, she will just turn up when you least expect to see her." I was finding our stay in Bumbuna still a bit difficult, actually very difficult. This was because my father or grandmother, or the usual uncle and aunties with familiar faces were nowhere to be found. Totally out of reach, no phone calls or text message, nothing back then. We were with complete strangers at that point in time. The place was packed with children our age, but it did not make it less daunting for me. It was a strange feeling and I found myself clamming up, saying less as the days went by.

Miss Kargbo called Fudia and I one evening and told us it was time for us to join in with the cooking process with all the other girls, not just to help out as we usually did, but to do the whole cooking by ourselves. We were going to start with cooking breakfast in the morning before church. This was not just cooking for a few people like we did in Magburaka, it was cooking for dozens of people. The pots were so big, the only time I had come close to a pot that size was in Fadugu with my grandmother. Now I had to cook on that big pot on my own. My God, I just wanted to get inside the pot and put the cover on. I somehow managed to cook the bulgur wheats in the morning and everyone ate it. I had watched and learnt from Georgiana, TK, Yama and the other girls. As they cooked in the mornings or evenings I would always be there to help out with the chores or sometimes just to listen to the big girls' conversations. Especially when they started talking about their boyfriends or whose boyfriend was going out with who, and who got snubbed on an occasion, the fights which went on, their talk was non-stop and it was all somehow so entertaining to me. Some days it would be ravioli, some days pasta, some days cassava or potatoes, or semolina porridge. And before I knew it, I was taking turns with cooking the dinner as well. I was doing the "big cook' as we used to call it. And as the name implied it was a very big cook indeed. The boys lived separately from us but we did all of the cooking for them. They knew the time to come for breakfast and dinner. They would all come to our place, eat and return to their place. That was when I got to see Baio sometimes. He looked like he had settled well with the other boys.

We would still see each other every day at church or when we were having dinner or breakfast. When the boys came to eat, they would do all sorts of things. They would tease us about the cooking. If your cooking was bad or not to their liking or not on time, they would let you know about it publicly. Cecilia, Vero and Christiana M were frequently on that list. I wouldn't say they were bad cooks, I will just say maybe they did not pay attention to their cooking. There were two Christianas in the house and we both had the same last name, we were only distinguished by our middle names or by our skin tone. They would call us "Christiana S", which was me, or "Christiana yahla" which was also me. The boys would also muck about or tease us about our looks. They used to call me flat waist or flat chest; I had not developed a womanly body like my mates. I felt lanky and lackadaisical amongst them. I learnt that word from my father, he would sometimes say to some of the students, "You lanky and lackadaisical." It was also when hanging around the big girls that I learnt how to take care of myself. One day I followed Vero to go and visit her boyfriend Safito. They sat together on the veranda while I sat opposite them. Well in fact, I was lying down on the bench putting both feet on the wall when suddenly Vero came and sat next to me. She had a serious face all of a sudden. Vero was looking at me directly as she said, "Put your feet down, we have to go home now." I was confused because we had only just arrived, we usually stayed longer.

So, I asked her, "Why are we going so soon?" and she said, "I think you have just entered womanhood." I was still confused, and I was looking at her blankly, then she said, "You have just started your periods, your menstruation has started." That was when it finally registered when she mentioned menstruation because we had done the menstrual cycle in school. At that point I was filled with embarrassment. I thought that if Vero had seen it, similarly Safito must have seen it too because they were sitting together. Vero helped me get up and she said, "We have to go now." It was when I got up that I felt something sticky and warm on my underwear. I did not say a word on the way home, I didn't know what to say or what to do. She took me to one corner when we arrived home, then she brought out some cloths and showed me how to use them. A few days after that initial stage to womanhood I was in the dormitory or our bedroom, when I heard Miss Kargbo calling for Fudia and me. I came outside and there she was, my mother. "You have to come with me quickly." She had reappeared exactly how Fudia said it would be. What was the matter, was Uncle ok? were my first thoughts.

But I did not say it out loud, we just followed her. Just over the road, not too far from the mission where we lived, she entered a house and we followed her inside. There he was looking back at us and smiling his slow smile. I was happy to see him, he looked much better than how I had left him, even though he was not the way he used to be. Two huge surprises at once. My mother spent a day or two in Bumbuna then she returned to Kolifaka, her place of work. Before she left, she told us that Uncle had been diagnosed with liver and kidney conditions and the doctors had told him to reduce or stop eating salt and maggi altogether. "Does that mean he is going to die?" I asked her.

"Well, everyone is going to die someday somehow, but if he does what the doctors say and takes his medications, only time will tell."

I was so happy for my father to be just within reach. The only downside was now Fudia and I had to cook his meals every day and also cook the "big cook" and breakfast at the mission when it was our turn to cook. We had to do a double cooking.

No wonder Baio and Fudia did not put their name down for St Matthew's secondary school. It was another change of dynamics when Baio chose to go to St Frances secondary school in Makeni. And Fudia also decided to go to Makeni at Tehco to learn gara tie-dying and catering. It was run by a woman called Civic.

I applied to go to Mathora secondary school for girls. It was a boarding school in Magburaka. I wanted to go there because most of my friends from RC Girls, my previous school, had always discussed the prospects of going to Mathora. And it was at Mathora where we went to take the exams. Our class travelled from Bumbuna to there. It was so surprising when I heard someone calling my name as we walked into the classrooms. I looked over, it was them, three of them, my old friends with a lot of other girls.

They were standing by the gates waving vigorously. "Mormi! Mormi!" they called to me when I turned around. I saw them mouthing and pointing downwards, in a way which suggested I should choose Mathora. I waved back and smiled. I definitely was not expecting to see any of them there. The place was rammed. All the other schools around that district were taking the exams on the same day.

My friends were already in secondary school, and I wasn't. It was because of the year which we spent in Fadugu without going to school. My second choice of school was Guadalupe secondary school for girls in Lunsar. I was accepted to both schools but my father told me, "Baio is going to Makeni, Fudia is going, if you go too, who is going to help me out now?" After taking that into account, and considering Lamin and Albert, there was no other option, the decision was to stay. Fudia and Baio left Bumbuna for Makeni, both living in different places. And yet again our lives took a different direction. I started attending St Matthew's secondary school. It was just a stone's throw from the mission. It was a mixed school for both boys and girls. And it was the only secondary school in Bumbuna.

My father taught agriculture, English language and sometimes biology in the school. I remember one time when he told us in class that if you wanted to get the nutrients from vegetables, especially leafy green vegetables, it was best to not overcook them.

When I cooked leafy green vegetables for him after school, it was a conscious decision from me to not overcook the vegetables. They were more or less raw as his food was delivered. A few minutes after delivering the food, he called my name with urgency in his voice. It could only be one reason for that type of call. And I knew exactly the reason for that particular call. "What is this?" He was holding the lead and pointing to the plasas. "Why is this plasas so raw? It is barely cooked." I smiled one of his slow smiles and said to him, "Well, I don't want to destroy all the vital nutrients from the vegetables, that is why I did not cook them through, or overcook them." To which he responded by taking off his glasses, looking at me, smiling back, and with that he said, "That studying you are doing in the classroom is not for my food ok," and we just burst out laughing. I took back the vegetables and cooked them in the usual way.

If it was not my turn to cook or do the housework in the mission, I would be at my father's place helping him with his laundry, wiping, cooking his meals or whatever chores needed to be done. The more we spent time together the more we became very close. As the time went on, I didn't find him as moody and mysterious as he used to be. I found him to be engaging and fun to be around. He was now calm and chatty. Sometimes I would rather sit with him and listen to his radio programmes like *Focus on Africa*.

Baio sent a message that he liked his school. He said he was doing well in class, even some of his best friends from Magburaka were also attending St Frances. The only thing he did not like was where he was staying because they made him do a lot of chores in the house. They even gave him stuff to go and sell after school, which meant he was having less time to do his schoolwork.

Fudia had also settled well and was excelling in the gara tie- dying in particular. Most times I missed them, I also missed our dogs and I missed our little adventures and the mischief with the other children in Magburaka. Would Cisi, Uncle and the three of us ever live under the same roof again? I was not sure, did I even want us to be under the same roof again? I was not sure about that either. I thought about Neptune our last dog, a female, who died before we left Magburaka. I thought about my grandmother. I was deep in my thoughts when my father reminded me to hurry back to the mission because it was almost time for the evening prayers.

At the end of any school term, both Baio and Fudia would return to Bumbuna and to the mission for the holidays. It was on one of those holidays that we decided to go and visit Cisi at her new station; she had told us in one of her visits how to get there. She said, "Get on the vehicles that are going to Bendugu and tell the driver to drop you at Kolifaka junction, once you are there, ask anyone, they will know where to find me. It is about a couple of miles from the junction to Kolifaka village itself." Almost everyone in the mission would go somewhere when the schools closed. We didn't want to be the only ones not going anywhere all of the time. We left to go and spend the holiday break with Cisi. The road was on top of a hill almost all the way through. Not just that, it was red clay and muddy with big gaps, potholes, splits all over the road at that time.

I had not seen anything like that on the other roads. At some point everyone had to get down from the vehicle so it could climb a specific area on the hill. I thought the car was going to roll backwards and flip over. After the push and pull on the road the car dropped us at the junction and we walked for about three to four miles to get to Kolifaka. It was smaller than Matotoka, way smaller. The people were really good to us, they brought us little gifts from the farms.

And in the evenings, they would put on the best cultural dance for women; it was one of the best dances I had ever seen. It was the way they beat the drums which went with the energetic exactness of the dancers. It was really enjoyable to watch and to experience. They did this dancing every night after they came back from their various farms.

They would dress up in cultural costumes and dance the night away under the heat of the dry season and the brightness of the moonlight. Sometimes they would light fires. One of the girls I became close to, told me they were getting ready and practising for their Bondo society which was set to take place in a couple of weeks. She said all the girls in the nearby villages would take part in a big dancing competition in front of all their potential husbands and their families. She was one of the best dancers.

I would sit there watching them dance until the crowd dispersed or until Cisi sent someone to come and collect me. One time I surprisingly found myself joining in. It was a very small village, but it was full of life, their marriage traditions were as entertaining as their Bondo society preparations. We could not stay long because the neighbour who helped out with my father's cooking would not separate the cooking for the salt. We soon returned to Bumbuna then spent a few days with Uncle before Fudia and Baio left for Makeni.

Chapter 12

By now the civil war, which had started from the southern part of the country, was spreading far and fast to other places. The rebels had taken hold of Kono and burnt most of the houses, maiming and killing most of the civilians. They also took children and women hostage. A lot of people came with all sorts of horrible encounters from the rebels. I silently prayed for Amadu and his sisters to be safe.

My father was getting worse, his feet were looking swollen and he was becoming more and more tired. We went to Mabesseneh hospital in Lunsar, where he was immediately admitted and the doctors said he should undergo surgery. My mother's elder brother, Uncle Paul Yayah Bangura, who we just called Uncle PY was living in Lunsar with his wife and children. I located them and discovered that Uncle PY was now working in Bo town, but his wife and children still lived there, a son and a daughter.

His wife taught in one of the primary schools. I told them the news that my father was going to be operated on the next day. I sat there and rested a bit; it took me a long time to find their house, and from the hospital to the town itself it was a hefty distance to walk under a very hot sun. After that I had some food and went to bed. My uncle's daughter Paulina was talkative, that was how we used to refer to her. She could talk non-stop. She wanted me to sit with her on the veranda and discuss all kinds of things from Guadalupe school to even boys. I could not; I spent less than ten minutes and went to bed.

Besides, I had to be in hospital first thing in the morning for my father's operation. By the time they came to collect him in the morning I was there by his side. I did not have to worry about what he could eat because he was told not to eat or drink before the operation. As soon as they took him in, I left again, and went back to my uncle's wife. Aunty Patricia, Paulina and I went to the market and I cooked some food for my father to eat after his operation.

I was sitting in one of the empty beds when they brought him out of the operation room. He was covered in all-white linen and there were tubes in his arms and some tubes in his mouth, he was not moving and his eyes where closed; it was frightening. The doctor explained to me that he would wake up after the anaesthetics had worn off. When he came around, he was shaking all over. One of the nurses ran to call the doctors. I don't know what they did but he was steady after a while and then he started to open his eyes slowly. He looked straight at me and all he could manage to say was, "Mormi." He looked exhausted as he lay there.

After a few minutes of talking to him, he fell back asleep. I tuned the radio in to his favourite radio channel and left it at that. He woke up again and sat up assisted by some pillows. I put some food on the plate, and he managed to eat a few spoons. At night I spread one of my lapa textiles on the floor and slept in the hospital. In a few days when he got stronger, I would sleep in Uncle PY's house until he was discharged and returned to Bumbuna. I was off school for a couple of days making sure he had all his medications on time. He recovered well from the operation and was back at school teaching.

The rebels had spread or were spreading from the eastern provinces to the northern parts of the country. We got information that the rebels had attacked Kambia. Most things got burnt down and people were killed, some captured. They took away my mother's younger stepsister and their last stepbrother. My mother told me this when she came on one of her brief visits to see us. Everyone in the country was worried and some fled from one part of the country to the next. Others left the country to seek refuge in neighbouring countries.

I must have been between thirteen to fifteen years old and my father had been in and out of hospital for the past six to seven years.

There were talks going around that it was time for us, the girls in the mission, to go into the Bondo society. Every girl child in our culture must undergo those initiations. They said it was for honour, culture and respect. Before they reached womanhood it was a must. I had a faint idea of what it entailed but not the whole details. You were not supposed to know anything about it until you were part of it. It was shrouded in one big secrecy. Father Berton, our family members and some of the elders in the town discussed it, then a date was set. My mother's aunt from Kambia was a member of the Degba or Soway committee; they were usually the ones who performed the female circumcision process. Arrangements were made for her to come and join the other members in Bumbuna since there were many girls from the township and from the mission so they might need more.

My father's younger sister, Fudia's mother, Aunty Sarah, also came with her two eldest daughters, Norkor and Fatu. Everything was going on so fast, my mother promised us not to worry, she told us everything would be fine, she said she had been for this occasion for a long time. "I have made arrangements to go to Conakry to shop for you," she explained. She promised to buy us gold jewellery and a lot of clothes. She told us this several times. "You must stay virgins, don't let men or boys tamper with you," she would say over and over. "If you are not a virgin during the time of the society, it will bring shame and disgrace to your family, if you are virgins, I am going to cook for you a whole chicken then put back all the giblets inside the chicken and stitch it together." She said that was the sign of virginity.

The day came, the town was packed, there were women everywhere, some dressed in traditional and cultural garments. They were singing and dancing all over the town. It was some kind of a big deal for the family as it signified their child or children were growing up or had grown up or were crossing over from childhood to adulthood.

When the day finally arrived, they assembled us all in one place, it was very early in the morning, the place was still dark when they woke us up and said it was time to go. They made us line up. The Soway and Degba were leading the crowd, and they were in full traditional garments. The family members were on both sides as we walked in the middle of them. It was fast and you could see the fear of the unknown in almost all of our faces. Like I said, I had a rough idea of what was going to take place, I was always around adults. But knowing about something and experiencing something are so not the same thing.

My mother was right in front of me, we kept walking until we reached the middle of nowhere in the bush. The space had been cleared up, a hut had been built and it had been fenced all around.

The Degba were standing at various points, they would call upon us one by one or grab us one by one. I was the first one to go, and it was my mother's aunt who performed the circumcision on me.

They pinned me down, some women sat on my chest, others held my feet and hands. There was no way out, you could not even move, you could hardly breath. The women were now singing very loudly as they beat the drums vigorously.

I suspected it was to prevent the cries and screams coming from us. By the time I could make sense of what was really going on, it was over. They had done it. I don't know how to explain it to you because I still don't know how to explain it to myself. I can only tell you it was part of our culture and traditions, it's the only way to put it. All of my family members went through it.

When it was over, the confusion and pain on everyone's faces could not be put into words. Slowly the cries faded away, the female circumcision was all done. The wounds had been dressed and we were given something to wrap around our waist. The women were now singing and clapping for us, or to us, they were singing songs and saying look at you, you are on your way to womanhood. I just sat there unable to move any part of my body. Fudia looked as though she wanted to conjure a magic trick and vanish into thin air. The women brought some soft white clay, mud clay called *woso* and rubbed it all over our faces, arms, backs, chests and feet.

They made all sort of patterns on our bodies. Another woman was saying to a girl just next to me as she applied the woso, "Now you can go to all our meetings and discussions because you are now part of us." All I was worried about was how to pee after all the dressing on the wound. It was stinging so bad, getting to your meetings was not my worry, I said to myself. And when I eventually peed it confirmed all the fears I had harboured. It was unbearable. We spent the next few days concentrating on healing, walking around and just getting used to what had just happened to us.

My mother's aunt who did the "deed" on me left the following day and went back to Kambia. My mother left two days after that. Aunty Sarah and my cousins left after a week. My mother said she was going for a few days to make sure everything was fine in her station then she would return back to us. She gave us injections to help heal the wound and to prevent tetanus. They started to make us do a lot of activities as we got better. Our first task in the mornings was to go to the river and have a wash before the men woke up. No boy or man was allowed to see or set eyes on us for the duration of the process.

They then taught us different activities; they taught us songs and we played until dinner time. Then it was time to do the other part of the initiations, I spoke to my mother's friend Tha-Nancy, I said to her, "Can you please send a message to Cisi so she can be present for the rest of the process." I did not want Fudia and me to be the only ones without close family members.

Although we had representatives from the mission it was not the same as having your mother on what looked like another big loop to jump. She agreed and even spoke to the elders to postpone the process for a few days until my mother returned. After a few days she still had not arrived, so they decided to carry on. In the evenings the women formed two long lines facing each other in the "Bondo Kantha" or "Bondo Bush". That was the name of the place we were now living.

The women held whips in their hands, the drumming and singing was at its loudest once more. And one by one we would go through the lines of women as they whipped us from both sides. After you reached the end of the line you had to return to where you started as they whipped you all the way back to the start line. As usual I was the first to be put through it because I was the *Rukoh*. The Rukoh was the one who went first in any of the activities. For example, when going to the river for a wash she stood in front and led the way. I ran as fast as I could trying not to fall. I had both hands over my face to protect my eyes and prevent marks or scars on the face.

That beating was not new to me even though the pain was something to lament on each time. Before we started secondary school, the senior boys and girls would organise something called drilling, another form of initiation, from primary school to secondary school. I don't know if it was part of the school curriculum because most schools did it.

Everyone wanting to attend that school had to take part in it. The process started very early in the morning with a three to four-mile run, then a roll in the mud and then two lines formed, which you had to pass between while being flogged from both sides. The only difference was this time it was all women. And as I was the first to always go in, I was not just the "guinea pig", I had to watch everyone else go through it. I stood there and relived it over and over again. That was really the pinnacle of pain.

As they were whipping Fudia from both sides, all I wanted to do was turn into some wild animal and chase them away. A lot of activities took place in and within the Bondo Bush, but you did not know until you were part it. I could not tell you that, I could tell you, the few days before we got out were really, how should I put it, a huge relief because all the major aspects were over and also because everyone was completely healed from their wounds, or they were almost healed. The older girls again used the fine white clay mud (woso) to draw fine patterns on our bodies. They taught us songs, dance moves, we ate, had naps, played all day.

That was it, all the major events were over, we had spent about a month or more in this process, it was time to get ready for the big reveal, it was time to be presented to the community as new women or new girls. It was time to see the outside world again. It was time for us to see boys and men, or for boys and men to see us, it was time to go back to school, time for some normality. Did I even know what normality was, had I ever experienced that which was normal? We were now new women or new girls. They called us *shama-fuw*. Father Berton sent people to do the shopping, to get us everything we needed for the big reveal.

He bought stuff for everyone that had taken part in the event. It usually involved putting on a lot of jewellery or beads on your neck, on both hands, round your waist and on your ankle. You were basically covered with everything shiny. Not to mention the Vaseline or *burn-pa-mine* they used to moisturise you from head to toe. You didn't wear clothes, just a piece of clothing to cover your waist and legs.

The breasts were on full display, some of us insisted on putting on a bra or another piece of clothing to cover up the breasted area. Somehow, we got away with it. My mother came back just a night or two before we were to go out. She brought us plenty of food stuff; I was not vexed at her because I was convinced her absence was due to her travelling to Conakry to go and buy us everything she said she was going to buy. The day came for us to go back into the world as new individuals. Before the dressing up began, my mother presented Fudia and me with a whole "stitch-up" chicken just as she had explained it to us. It tasted really good that morning. There were the signs of virginity. Everyone started to get dressed.

I could not find my mother; she must have gone to get us the things she went to buy from Conakry I said to Fudia and she nodded in agreement. One of the women Yama came and gave us what everyone was supposed to wear, some added it to what their family members had already got for them. I still refused to put anything on, "We are waiting for Cisi," Fudia responded as they kept urging us to get dressed. We had to be at the front for the big reveal and we had not put on anything. "Right, it's time to get going everyone, Rukor come and take the lead, yield the Degba."

My mother reappeared empty-handed. "Cisi, where are the things from Conakry?" we asked her.

"I did not have time to go to Conakry, I will still go, don't worry just put on this for now, ok." Yama one of the women who had been constantly urging us to get dressed came rushing to us. "I have been telling you two to get dressed for quite some time and now you are holding everyone up, they are waiting for you so we can leave." She was hanging and putting stuff on us as she was speaking. "I could have dressed you up properly, I kept asking but you insisted on waiting for your mother." She kept saying almost the same thing. "You can't go out like this especially when you are the ones standing in front and leading the way."

We rushed and somehow made it to the line with Fudia who was the *Burah*. The Burah was the one after the Rukor. One of the women came to have a quick glance at everyone. She gave instructions, then we started moving slowly this time. They were now singing songs and beating on the drums. They held cloth-like material to form a canopy over our heads. This was to prevent the sun from hitting us directly, some were fanning us. The whole town came out to see us, meet us and to greet us. We walked from one end of the town to the other. And all the while I had yet to recover from the let-down, deflation, and disappointment I had just received. It quickly turned into annoyance and I started asking myself, who does that, how could you, why did you? It was a fine line between disappointment and annoyance, one of them definitely led to the other. I just wanted the parade to be over so I could find somewhere to go and lie down. But no, we had to go round the town so everyone could see us, wave at us, or cheer for us. The singing, eating and dancing went on till the late evening. And that was it, everything went back slowly to the way it was.

Chapter 13

The first thing I did when everything about the Bondo had quietened down was speak to my father. I told him I wanted to go to the city Freetown for a break, I wanted to get away from all of it. Fudia went back to Makeni. I asked Uncle about going for a visit to my mother's younger sister who lived in the city. I had just turned sixteen. He agreed and told me not to stay too long. I had been to the city before on holidays: the first visit I stayed in Porty around the east of the city, the other time it was in Congo across to Uncle Usman Tose's and then Lumley to Aunty Sarah's. This time I decided to visit Aunty Baby who sold in Dofcort; the mother of Lamin whom I was in the mission with. Lamin and Baio always tried to outdo each other, they were both very clever and could be very competitive. If one took first place in class, the other one would also try and not only take first place but do so with a higher mark.

Very early in the morning I left with the first vehicle starting the journey to Freetown; it was just me this time. I didn't know where Aunty Baby lived, but I knew where she sold. The three of us had visited her. There was a time we came for a holiday and stayed with Aunty Sarah in Babadori Lumley. As long as she was still doing business within that market vicinity, I would find her because like her elder sister, my mother, she would not be difficult to locate.

Aunty Baby, also known as Tha-Baby, was chatting to a customer as I approached. "This cassava dae bos?" the woman asked her, and my aunt responded, "Mama Krio, this jus put am na hot water E dae bos, pow, E nor need for boil sef, even if you put am inside flax E go cook." I shook my head, that was definitely Aunty Baby I said to myself. The lady was asking my aunt if the cassava could cook well, and my aunt said yes, all you had to do was put it in some hot water then it would cook, without even having to reach boiling point. She went on to say, even flax water would cook the cassava. As she said this, all the other women around her burst out laughing. I was laughing too. After the transaction with the woman, she looked up and saw me smiling at her. She stood up, and said, "School girl, how are you doing?" "Is everything ok, how is my sister, how is Lamin, is your father alright, what has happened, why are you here, what are you doing here?" She was spraying questions at me and looking worried. She was not expecting my visit, it was totally unannounced. "You worry too much Aunty; everyone is fine I just needed a change of environment after the Bondo," I answered.

"That is why you are looking all grown-up, am so sorry I missed it, I really wanted to be there but I had a lot of perishable goods to sell at the time, so how did it all go?" She held my hand. "Come and sit down." Then she finally relaxed, the smiled had returned back to her face. "Isiah," she called her eldest daughter, "come and take your sister to the house." She brought out some money and handed it to her. "Buy food product so you two can cook ok." It was a three-room flat around mountain court.

In the morning, Aunty wanted Isiah and me to stay at home while she went to sell in the market, but there was no way I was going to do that: to miss all the fun, camaraderie and banter in the marketplace. I didn't think so because that was the most exciting part for me.

Between those market women and their customers, you could learn so much and laugh so much. We left with her and when we arrived at the market, she told me, "If you need to go to the bathroom while you are here, just cross the road and go to that house." Aunty Baby showed me around the market. "You remember Yamariama fula from Matotoka don't you?"

"Yes, I remember," I answered.

"One of her daughters, Tha-lamrana lives there. They have a running tap in the back as well."

I nodded in acknowledgement. By noon I followed Isiah to go and use the bathroom. As I was coming out of the bathroom, I heard a voice saying, "Amadu if you see those new trainers in the shop, you will like them." I looked up, it was Baba Alie, then I turned around to see who he was talking to, and it was Amadu. He was looking directly at me with his mouth half opened. Our eyes met and all we could do was look at each other both unable to speak or didn't know what to say. It was the same Amadu from Matotoka, and this was the first time of seeing him since they had left with their mother. How come he was looking so big and tall? I asked myself. "Mormi," he finally called my name and brought me from my initial shock. "Amadu," I responded.

He stepped closer to me and held my hand. "You have grown a lot."

"You have grown too," I answered. We exchanged pleasantries and he asked me to come inside the house to greet Aunty Lamrana, his mother's elder sister. I did. "You can come to the house any time, am mostly around at this time," he said to me before we left. He can talk, he can smile, he was warm and welcoming, what had happened to that grumpy distant boy? I kept thinking to myself.

When we got back to the house that late afternoon, all I could think about was Amadu; he must have been around eighteen years old by then. Now I had a personal matter, which was beginning to interest me. I was much more enthusiastic about going to the marketplace. I looked forward to a certain individual who was starting to make the visit extra special.

The next day around the same time, I went to the house pretending to go and use the bathroom and made sure Isiah did not come with me. After greeting everyone, we went and sat in the living room and chatted for some time before I returned back to the stall. Some days he would come around to the stall and pretend to buy something from the nearby tables. He would make sure I saw him. And just like that my bladder needed emptying. My peeing had become frequent. "Isiah let's go and use the bathroom," I told my cousin.

"Am not going, I don't feel like using the bathroom, just say you want to go and see Amadu."

I rolled my eyes at her and she laughed a laugh that said ha! Got you! And I said to myself, am I that predictable? I was only a few years older than Isiah.

On one occasion, as we sat in the living room, some of his cousins would pass by making teasing sounds or they would just look at us and smile teasingly. He got up and said, "Come, let's go." He then led the way to their own room downstairs and he closed the door behind us. He asked me if I was going to be living with Aunty Baby permanently. "No, am just here for a break," I said. He told me he had attended Magburaka government secondary school for boys (MGSS), the same school my father used to teach at, and he was now attending St Edwards secondary school in the city. And I told him about our moving to Bumbuna.

The conversation quickly changed when he said, "I have always wanted to hold you, do you know that?" I wanted to say yes, I know, or what are you talking about? or I didn't have a clue. The words would not come out, I just smiled instead. Why was I feeling like this, what was happening to me?

After a while, well, well, well, my goodness, this had turned out to be an eventful trip indeed.

Before I left for Bumbuna we promised to write to each other.

My father had had another episode with his health and I felt so bad and so guilty for leaving him for those few days. He said to me "It's ok, am fine I just don't want to die when you are not here."

"You are not going to die Uncle, you are going to get well," I responded. We took another visit to the hospital and they said what he had had was a mild heart attack.

They gave him different medications, sometimes I had to give him the injections myself. After a few months he went for another operation: not heart surgery, it was something else. We returned back and everything seemed to be going well for about two months.

By now the rebel war was spreading rapidly. The rebels were taking over more towns and villages. It was all so dramatic the way they spoke on the focus on Africa, especially one of the rebel leaders who was commonly known as Maskita, that is "mosquito" in English.

He would say things such as, "We are taking over, no one is going to stop us, no bush shaking, any bush that shakes we will comb that area." It was on one of those listening times when Uncle told me to always broaden my horizon. "Don't just limit yourself on certain things," he said, "read the newspaper, listen to the radio, and listen to experienced elders." He was turning to numb the radio trying to get a clear sound when he spoke, "You will always learn something from anyone."

His health was failing him more and more as the time went on. I could clearly see the look on the doctors' faces on our last visit to Mabeseneh hospital. When the tests came back, I knew it was not good, I could feel it, but I was not ready for what was about to come. They said if he had one more heart attack it could be fatal. We left and returned to Bumbuna. It was the holidays. Baio, Fudia and Cisi all came to spend some time with us in Bumbuna. The morning before they were to leave, my father kept calling on us and asking, "Where is my food, hurry up, am hungry?" I was completely surprised, he had never demanded for his food in that manner before. We rushed and cooked the food; we took his own out then added salt and maggi to ours.

After we had all eaten, we sat on the veranda discussing. He told us a story about two friends who lived in a village, both of them were building their own house and both of them did not have enough roofing material. So late at night, when one of the friends was sleeping, the other one went and stole all of his friend's roofing materials and put them on his own roofing. When the friend asked about his stolen roofing materials, he denied taking his friend's materials.

The following night a strong wind came, and it took off all the roof on the stolen man's house and placed it on the other roof which it was stolen from. We all laughed as he concluded. Some of us asked how was that possible? And others said that would teach him a lesson, and others said that would never happen in real life. My father said nothing, he was just smiling to himself.

Baio and Fudia left for Makeni, and about half an hour later Cisi also left for Kolifaka. Uncle said to me, "Well now that I have eaten, am feeling a bit tired, am going to lie down and have a rest."

I said, "No problem." I stayed on the long bench on the veranda where the five of us had been sitting. I didn't know how long I had slept out there. But all I remembered was when I felt a tap on my shoulder the sun was shining brightly on the veranda and it was blinding me on my face.

I got up and put a hand over my face to try and see who was tapping me. It was Mr Kanu and Veronica, the next-door neighbours. They were kneeling over me. "I heard your father scream, I went to check on him, I have called to the sister (nun) who is a nurse, I think he has had another heart attack," Mr Kanu explained to me. I just got up and walked towards my father's bedroom. Every step felt like a lead on my legs. It was the first time I had ever felt a lump in my throat. I could not move the lump from there for I could not speak, it was more than painful.

He was motionless on the bed. I sat by him and managed to lift him into a sitting position. I hugged him and tried to call him so he would wake up. The lump was still there so I just rocked from side to side. I just sat there holding him close. Not so soon, not today, not my Uncle, not my father, I was trying to say out loud. Yet the words could not come out. They had gone to call for help and a car to rush him to hospital. The nuns came, one, the nurse, checked his pulse. "He still has a very faint pulse," she explained. I could feel his body weight changing as I still held him. He suddenly felt very heavy. They took him from me and lay him back on the bed. The room was now packed with people, the car came to take him away. The sister said to Mr Kanu, "It is too late; he will not make it to the hospital." He was gone, Uncle was dead. He was forty-eight years old and he had been sick for eight years or more. I was sixteen years old. Father Berton sent a car to go and collect my mother, and arrangements were made to take his body to Fadugu. We picked up Baio and Fudia from Makeni and continued to Fadugu.

It was night, as the car pulled up the whole place erupted with screams. People came from every part of the town, crying from every corner of the house. My grandmother was sitting on a woven-mart on the floor and they lay the body near to where she was sitting. She was calling my father's name repeatedly. "Why would you leave me? Why would you leave your children?" More cries erupted.

That was the first time I heard myself or felt myself cry. Mami Iye gave us water and consoled us. I went to my grandmother and just sat by her side. I could not say a word. What do I say to a woman who just lost her first child, the child who was supposed to bury her? Not the other way around, for a mother to bury their child, it was against the law of nature. He was buried at Kakendema next to his father's grave.

Chapter 14

My mother had moved from Kolifaka to another station called Margban. It was far away from Bumbuna and it was smaller than Kolifaka. There were no roads for a car to get to Margban village at that time. You had to travel to a town called Mile 91 and then walk the rest. The distance felt longer than Magburaka to Matotoka.

The road was narrow and slippery, it felt like it had not been walked on since God knows when. Fudia, Baio and I had no idea it had been raining in the other village and there was a river which was to be crossed from one side to the other. The river had been overflowing when we arrived. It was the only route we knew.

The only choice we had was to turn back and return to Bumbuna, but it was already starting to get dark and we might not even get a car to take us to Bumbuna around that time. That option was near impossible. Or we could just risk it and venture ahead in the risen river. We had a few discussions with ourselves and agreed with option two which was to cross. We stepped in, it was getting deeper as we moved forward, the water was now around my chest, and Baio said we should go back, the water was above his chest. "Who is there, stop right there, do not take another step or all of you are going to drown?"

It was a man paddling a canoe. "What are you doing here at this time of the night, there is a current swiping people around that area you are standing in?"

"We are going to visit our mother the nurse who has just been transferred to Margban," I answered.

"Ahh yes, I heard they have a nurse for the first time." It was a very small canoe, so he crossed with us one after the other. He told us it was not too far anymore but the road it was not good to walk on at this time because of the rain. We thanked him and he was gone.

I slipped and fell down more than three times by the time we got there. The spirogyra was visible on the road, it was raining non-stop. We were wet and shaking, I was feeling feverish when we got to the final destination.

Cisi was not there, she had gone to a nearby village to treat someone. As usual I said to myself. The man, who was her trainee, checked my temperature and it was high; he gave me an injection in the buttocks and some tablets. When I woke up in the morning the fever had gone down a little bit. I was feeling much better, but my bum cheek was burning like fire. I showed my mother, and she gave me some paracetamol tablets and said it would be fine. After a few days the place where he had injected me had swollen up a bit. My mother said it looked like an abscess then gave me antibiotics. It looked to be going down.

"How come you are moving every time, why is it that every place you move to is smaller and more difficult to get to than the last?" Baio and Fudia were laughing, Cisi was laughing too, but I wasn't; it was starting to annoy me.

"Because the people in those villages are the ones who seriously and desperately need health and medical attention, they need care and support too," she responded simply.

Well, you do have a point I wanted to say but I did not for fear she might disappear into a village that was unreachable. Instead, I said, "You are not the only nurse, must it always be you? All the friends you trained together with are working in big towns and villages, you are always moving from bush to *kanth*." The three of them were laughing again. Kanth just meant a thicker bush in my mother's language. At least there were no temper tantrums which I was expecting and was already prepared for. You could tell just by the way I was standing. "Come," she called to me and made a gesture for me to sit by her side.

"Am doing this for you. I know it is difficult on you, you might not see it now but one day you will see it." She paused and pushed some wood on the fire. "As am looking after other people's children, God is going to look after you." I nodded blankly. Can't wait to see it I said to myself. When we got back to Bumbuna the abscess reappeared in three different places very close to the other. I still have the scars on my bum cheek. I visited Cisi again in Margban, this time it was only me.

Then Cisi moved to another station called Kayasi. Kayasi was a small town, but it was much closer to Bumbuna and it was on one of the main roads from Bumbuna to Makeni. You could get a car from Bumbuna and it would drop you right in front of my mother's house.

One morning, I was doing the sweeping in the mission when I saw a lot of people carrying their belongings on their heads. They were heading in the direction of Binkorlor, the direction to where my mother was. I had already guessed the answer before I asked one of them what was going on. And they confirmed my worst nightmares.

The rebels were close by, they had overtaken a nearby town, Tonkolili. Since Bumbuna was the next big town in that area it was evident that it would be their next target. And considering how rapidly they were moving, the rebels could be in Bumbuna sooner than expected. By the time I returned to the dormitory the news had gone around. Panic and commotion had taken hold. For all I knew they might show up from the backyard by the time I had found Lamin, if they were not in the backyard already. Everyone was running helter-skelter.

I gathered my books, picked up a few clothes, grabbed Lamin by the hand and we left heading towards Kayasi. It was a big crowd, all having only one goal which was to save their lives, or to save the lives of their family members. Every one or two miles the bag would become heavier, so I would remove a few books or clothes and toss them to the ground. As we carried on walking, I thought about all the Salcost workers who worked on the hydroelectricity. I thought about my mother's younger brother Mordu who also worked at Salcost.

I thought about the boy Tinka who they matched us with in the mission, how he followed me and how he harassed my life if I spoke to any other boy. One time I was talking to this boy, and I had no idea he was behind me; all I could remember was getting kicked at my feet and I was on the floor. How he would follow me each time we went dancing at the court barray. I thought about the sporting activities, how they made me do almost every event, like the 100 metres, the 400 metres the 800 metres and the hurdles all in one day, how I almost passed out. It was really thrilling. My father's room had not been touched and all his things were still in it. I knew he had been buying gold from the gold miners, I saw him look at it so many times, I knew where it was kept but I could not risk going back to that house.

I thought about the times we spent Christmas Day with Father Berton and all the Italian workers at Salcost. How enthralled I was to see all that food in one place, at the same time, and I was engulfed by the way it was layered out, how big the lobsters and shrimp were, the chocolate, cakes, sweets, biscuits and fruits. How we would add alcohol to our Kokkola drinks when father was not watching. If he had suspected anyone of drinking alcohol, he would randomly go to the table where you were sitting and call you out. He would make you stand on one leg for a few seconds. If you wobbled that meant you had been drinking or you were over the limit.

He would then ask you to go and wait in the car. Especially the boys, they would drink a lot and they would talk and laugh so loudly, they would bang on the tables and make fun of each other. He made one of the boys wait in the van. By the time we had finished and got back to the van, Saidu was throwing up. Imagine if he were to vomit in the hull, in front of everyone. It was really a fun and a warm welcoming Christmas Day celebration for us all. I thought about our outings to the Bumbuna waterfalls. We would cook all types of party food and spend the whole day in front of the water, watching it fall from the rocky hill to the river, it was so loud you could hardly hear the music which we took with us and played on huge sets of speakers. I thought about how we would try so hard to speak the Italian language in order to communicate with the guests who would visit us from Italy. They would stay for some time and could not speak a word of English, especially Laurena, a cousin of Father Berton. She would visit us regularly with other family members. I can barely put two words together now.

We were almost at Kayasi when I heard the sound of a vehicle approaching. It was already packed and moving so slowly. I picked Lamin up and threw him inside the vehicle. He landed on top of people's laps. With one hand carrying whatever was left of my luggage, I held on with the other hand by the back door of the vehicle.

Cisi was standing outside Kayasi when we pulled up for the driver to have a break. We greeted her and quickly narrated the series of events. I told her I was not stopping because you could never be too careful, they might be everywhere before day broke. I told her to come with us, but she was adamant about staying put. So, we left. I slept at the nurse house in Binkorlor and continued to Freetown the following day. Fudia had graduated and was now living with her parents in Freetown; their place was so overcrowded. Father Berton had taken a place in Kissy duck yard for the bigger boys and girls who were in sixth form. But he was in Italy recovering from a knee surgery when all this disarray was going on.

I went to Kissy duck yard a week after I arrived in Freetown and Miss Kargbo was already there. She told me father had been worried about all of us. The place was spacious with electricity and running water; most of the people from the mission in Bumbuna were there so I decided to stay with them.

Bumbuna was burnt down by the rebels, some were captured, others killed, the same unfathomable horror all over the country. What if my father had still been alive, how could we have coped? Fadugu had also fallen. My grandparents' house, and every memory of my grandmother, burnt to the ground. My grandmother was relocated to Freetown and stayed with her daughter Aunty Sarah. Thank goodness she got out alive.

The schools in Freetown were over their capacity. Our names were on the waiting list. They said we could be waiting for a whole year before someone could be offered a place at Bishop Johnson secondary school. The school father wanted for us was St Joseph convent but they had a waiting list for God knows when. St Helena had a place and it was within walking distance. I started attending St Helena after a couple of weeks. Some days I would go and see Aunty Baby mainly to check on Lamin and to make sure he was still going to school. His truancy was becoming too much.

The market women were packing up to close for the day and I was rushing to go and get a taxi to Kissy duck yard. It was still around Guard Street, not too far from his aunt's house. There he was coming from the opposite direction. I did not know what to say neither did I know what to do. It was Amadu. I wanted to pretend I had not seen him but it was too late for that. He stopped right in front of me, we were now face to face. He was looking at me smilingly. I almost smiled back, then my mother's words came crashing into my head. She was saying one of her favourite phrases, "behaviour oh behaviour", which I replaced with "composure oh composure"; it was no time to be nice or friendly, remember you are pissed off with him, I reminded myself. "Did you get the letter I wrote to you?"

With a broad smile, he said, "Yes, I did." He went on. "I replied. What is the matter, did you not like the reply?"

"Well, I did not get your reply. I have to go, or I will be late." Then I walked past him. When I turned back to look, he was standing there with both hands stretched out and his mouth open with a puzzled face.

The gate closed at 7 pm at Kissy duck yard. If you were not in by then, you would have to explain yourself, get a telling off, or the gate man would simply refuse to open the gate as instructed. I did not tell Amadu all of that, I just walked on, all because I did not receive his letter.

It had always fascinated me how one moment you didn't even think about an individual and the next moment they were all you could think about. I could not block him out of my head, my fighting the impossibilities and it was futile.

It took me two days to finally build up the courage to go and see him so we could maybe make up or just have a civilised conversation. With my best clothes on, I climbed the stairs to their house. One of his elder cousins Lamrana was sitting on the veranda. She called my name as we greeted each other and sat together. "Oh, Mormi, you just missed him."

"Miss what?" I asked.

"Amadu. He travelled yesterday to the UK." Stunned was an understatement. I was unable to even look up at her let alone think, everything went blank. After a brief moment I said, "It's ok. I came to visit Aunty Baby and decided to drop by."

I got up and said, "I have to go before it gets late," and I left. It was almost a year since Amadu had left for the United Kingdom; there was no communication between us. Yet sometimes I would find myself thinking of him. I was attending the Bishop Johnson secondary school by then. It was a mixed school with both boys and girls.

Bishop Johnson was bigger, with more friendliness for me compared to St Helena. What I am really trying to say is most of the boys and girls at BJ as we simply called it were more outgoing. I made plenty of friends. It was easy to get on with almost everyone in my class. My type of crowd definitely. Winston Williams and Samuel Manages were my besties and Fatu and Daphne were the accomplices to be more precise. I started noticing this boy who always hung around school. He would be there during break times or during home time. He had no uniform on, so he must not have been an active student. I later found out he was an ex-pupil who had just left or finished school. He would come too sometimes. He would talk to Samuel or Winston; that was how or when I took notice of him for the first time.

And sometimes he joined us as we walked outside of the school gates. That was also how we started talking. When we were outside the gate, we would all go in our different directions. He would then walk with me and stand with me until I got a taxi to go home. That quickly became a regular pattern. Girls started making remarks and forming little groups, talking loudly, some even laughing or just doing something to be noticed when they saw us together. He would say to just ignore them, and I asked him one time, "Girlfriend?" looking in the direction of one of the girls. "No." I made a face, and he said, "Was, long time ago," then we both laughed.

His slightly worried face then subsided. "Are you sure of it?" He got so close to me and leant over me, I could feel his breath on my face. With that he said calmly, "Yes Christiana, am very sure." He was way taller than me, he played in the school basketball team: that was why he was always in and around the school. He was waiting on the other boys so they could all go and practise together after school. He then held my hand and said, "Come, let me find you a taxi, I know how to make the taxi drivers stop." After school it was impossible to get transportation, every *poda poda* and taxi was full, it could sometimes take more than an hour to get one.

I later found out he had dated or was even dating a lot of girls in the school. If I asked him, he would deny it or simply say not anymore. He asked me if I was coming to the school bonfire night. I told him I was not sure because the gates to the house closed at 7 pm. I asked for permission to attend. The bonfire was lively, it was held in the school compound. Most of my classmates attended, we hung out together and Ladner left us and joined his friends, and then returned. "We should go clubbing sometimes, you will like it," he told me one day.

"That is definitely not going to be allowed," I told him.

"Well, you don't have to tell them," he responded with a conspiratorial laugh. "Don't worry, next week around 9 pm I will pick you up."

"How? You have seen the fence haven't you? You know very well you are not allowed to come in."

"Just put some clothes in a bag and wait for me around 9 pm at the end part of the fence."

When everyone was busy doing one thing or the other, I heard a faint whisper, it was him and a friend, "Send the bag over." I did, and he caught it.

I climbed on an old stool then both of them got me over the fence. With only tiny scratches from the barbwire, we left. He took me to his house where we spent some time, changed and left for the club. It was almost 12am when we got to the club and it was jam-packed, to its fullest capacity. The club was called Rumours at that time. We danced till about 3am. By the time he came to drop me back at Kissy duck-yard, where I was living, the time was 5–6am in the morning. I could not jump back over the fence because there was no one to catch me, except if I wanted to end up with a broken leg. We sat by the fence waiting for the gate to open around 7am.

We heard movement and he said goodbye and left. I entered the gate holding my shoes on my hands tippy-toeing inside. "Where are you coming from?" It was Miss Kargbo. They kicked me out for rule breaking or staying out all night. I went to stay with my aunt. My aunt's place to the school was very far; it was a long way to travel every day. I would spend the whole day travelling to school and from school.

It required changing to two to three transportations each way. Fudia was now living with her mother and she was not feeling well by the time I came to stay with them. The place was so small; because of the war in the country almost every family member was now in Freetown at that time as Freetown was more or less the only place which had not been attacked at that point.

I decided to visit father in his office and explained my predicaments to him. I went back and promised to not stay out again. Every day that passed by, I was getting sick of the rules and the routine. I didn't have any desire to become a nun anymore. I now wanted to do things mates my age were doing: things like going clubbing with some of my friends, Fatu and others, or going to watch movies. All of the above was not allowed. If we wanted to do any activities, it had to be planned, managed and supervised. And clubbing or going to the movies were definitely not on the agenda. Ladner did get me into a lot of trouble, or shall I say, I got myself into so much trouble. I packed by bags and left for the last time. I had decided to not stay at Kissy duck-yard again. Father did everything he could for me to return but it was to no avail. My mind was completely made up. I crashed with my aunt. I spent a lot of time with Ladner after school.

One day as we sat by the window in his living room looking over the street and listening to music, he said to me, "You like your rucksack, don't you?" He was referring to my school bag.

"What is wrong with it?" I asked him back and went on to say, "There is nothing to like about it, it's just a school bag." "Mama am begging you calm down, am just saying, it is not very girly, you should get one of the new-style school bags which most of the girls are carrying."

"No thanks, am good and am not most of the girls, ok, you can go and hang out with them since you like their school bags so much," I answered back.

"Am going nowhere, don't get jealous."

He laughed and pulled me close. I poked him on the chest and made a face. "Am not jealous." He made a face and we both laughed again. That got me thinking about where we had grown up or the way we grew up, how you only wore what you wanted, what you could afford, what you could manage to lay your hands on, or what could fit you. For example, when we had clothes, or if and when the clothes arrived for everyone to share amongst themselves, they were usually in bulk form or huge piles. You only got what you were able to get hold of, what you got offered and, in most cases, they were too big or too small, too long and too short. The shoes could be so tight your last two toes felt like they were on fire. The latest styles and latest fashions were definitely not my thing. The next day, when he came to escort me into a taxi as usual, he was clutching something in his hand. He smiled his daft smile and handed it to me. I looked and it was something similar to the bags the girls were using. I handed it back to him and told him I already had a bag.

"Why you tan so ba?" he said to me.

"Na so are tan," I responded back.

He was saying to me, "Why are you acting like this?" "That is exactly how am acting," I responded.

"Christiana, you are a stubborn girl, come let's go."

He stopped a taxi and I got in. Just as the taxi was moving off, he threw the bag on my lap and ran off. One of the girls in our rooms saw it and said that it was a good school bag and that relaxed me a bit. Well after some time I used the new school bag and thanked him. To which he said, "I wish you would let me do more Christiana."

"You have made enough trouble for me already, thank you." We giggled knowing the late-night incidents I was referring to.

Fudia was still not feeling well. We took her to Connaught hospital. The doctor gave her some queeny tablets; they were light yellow in colour, and he gave her a queeny drip. After a few minutes, she said, "I can hear a humming sound in my ears, my ears are ringing." That was the start of what was to be a tumultuous, harrowing time. As the days passed, her body felt better but she was slowly losing her hearing.

"Mormi, I can't hear, I can't hear you," she would say to me. I explained this to the doctor, and he said the queeny medicine did that sometimes, it would clear up eventually, but it never cleared up. She was discharged, and I took her home. Fudia made her tie - dye and she would sell them, then she opened a small stall selling every day essential stuff. Because of the health of Fudia and the change of address, I started to see Ladner less. We had finished our GCSE, and I was not going to school anymore; no one did because there was nothing to do. He lived not too far from the school.

Chapter 15

As the rebels took over most of the towns and cities in the provinces, the military also overthrew the then lead government of Joseph Saidu Momoh in 1992. The coup d'état was headed by Valentine Strasser. On 20 April, they formed the NPRC (National Provisional Ruling Council). The NPRC was in government for about four years before it was toppled.

We woke up one morning and there was pandemonium in the city; there were military men in their military vehicles going up and down the city. It was quickly announced on the radio that another coup d'état had taken place. It was one of the military men within the Strasser government who had staged a palace coup in 1996. Valentine Strasser was forcefully outed by members of his own government. All the while, the rebels kept advancing into the city and they were destroying everything in their path. The instability had taken hold of the whole country. People were moving from place to place: displacement was the order of the day.

My mother had been displaced also and was now working at King Haman Road hospital in Freetown. She was staying with a friend on Hill Cut Road. I would visit her regularly because it was closer to where I was living. It was when I visited her one evening, that I overheard them discussing the shortages of everyday commodities like sugar and salt to some parts of the towns and villages. Some of the towns had been completely cut off. The rebels controlled some places and the army was in control of other places. He said the people had been harvesting a lot of palm oil but there was no one to buy palm oil from them. He was a captain officer by then. Fudia and I bought a lot of the food items: salt, sugar, maggi, onions.

We used almost every penny we had between us and gave it to the captain. After a couple of weeks or months, he brought us back plenty of palm oil in exchange for the items he took. Palm oil and other food items were also scarce in the city due to the cut-offs. We sold our palm oil for a good price and we started looking for a place to rent for ourselves; we were practically living on top of one another at my aunty Sarah's place. We found a one-bed flat not too far from Lumley where my aunt lived. The place was called Wilberforce Village. It was a one-car stop journey from Lumley to Wilberforce. Or if you knew the area really well, you could use another route to walk there. Fudia, Baio and I moved into the one-bed flat. The house was fenced and secured. Finally, the three of us were back together, living under the same roof after a very long time of living in different places. Fudia and I slept in the bedroom while Baio slept in the living room. We were still waiting for the GCSE results to come out.

I started going to Conakry, buying women's clothes and selling them to my friends, especially to my church friends. They would always compliment me on what I was wearing and I told them I was selling clothes. Fudia and I spent a lot of time in church as well. I grew up in a Roman Catholic setting, but I liked this church which a friend had invited me to. It was called Jesus is Lord Ministries, simply known as Mami Dumbuya. Most people called the church Mami-Dubuya because that was the name of the female founder. By the end of 1996 there was an election and the military handed over power reluctantly to a democratically elected government. The war was still going on, but things seemed to be calming down in the city with all the military coups. There was not much for us to do. I went to almost every service in the church, including the all-night prayer service. The war was advancing rapidly. So many people were fleeing to neighbouring countries.

Just few years into the Ahmad Tejan Kabbah lead government, there was yet another coup from the military. The elected government of Tejan Kabba had been overthrown by another group of soldiers and their leader was Johnny Paul Koroma. Their government was called the AFRC (Armed Forces Revolutionary Council). Tejan Kabba fled to Guinea Conakry and plotted his return back to power. With the help of the ECOMOG in 1998 the AFRC government, which was led by Johnny Paul Koroma, was destabilised by Tejan Kabba. It was awful. The ECOMOG who came to reinstate him were based at the Lungai international airport. To get to Freetown you had to cross the sea by boat, ferry or helicopter. The ECOMOG made a base around the Lungai area and launched weapons and shelled missiles into the city all day and all night. The military responded with their own firing. Us, the civilians, were caught in the middle. Tejan Kabba refused to back down, saying that even if he had to kill everyone, he would return to power. He went on to say that even if there were only chickens left in the country, he would return back to power. So many of us heard him say that on an interview with the BBC.

That was how terrible the situation was. Some days the alpha-jet would drop bombs. The jet would pass so low the houses would shake; well, your whole body would shake. I don't remember being afraid, maybe it was because the focus was on how to stay alive. Survival instinct, the will to live, may have taken over the "fear". Where we lived in Wilberforce was also where the largest army barracks was located therefore the barracks was targeted. They were doing everything to destabilise the army. Tejan Kabba and his ECOMOG were doing whatever they could just to get rid of the army, at the detriment of the innocent civilians who had nowhere to go. They shelled the city of Freetown all day long. On one occasion a bomb was dropped just two houses from where we lived. It killed Hazel, an 18-year-old girl.

She was the only daughter of a next-door neighbour. A fragment got her as she was trying to take cover from their house in the basement. Seeing the injured, hearing the screams, and knowing that you were trapped with nowhere to run to or nowhere to hide, there was only one way now, you lived with the atrocities, or you got killed by a bullet, a fragment, or hunger and disease. You couldn't go back to the villages and towns outside of the city, the rebels controlled most of those places. It was too late to seek refuge in a neighbouring country by then. All we could do was pray for it to be over, wait for it to be over and hope to still be alive when it was over.

The jet was still coming around our area every day and it would pass so low you could feel your whole body vibrate. Some days it would pass repeatedly as if it was going to drop a bomb at any point. Those were the days we would go without food. Other days we had a few spoons of boiled rice with nothing on it or may be just a few sprinkles of palm oil on the boiled rice. The market was closed, no one was selling food stuff, but if you knew where a market woman lived, you could go to their house and maybe get a few items. I ventured out on one occasion and quickly regretted my action. There were checkpoints everywhere, armed men pointing guns at you and asking you all types of questions. We had the Economic Community of West African States Monitoring Group (ECOMOG) peacekeeping force, the local militia men known as the Kamajors, the Armed Forces Revolutionary Council soldiers (AFRC), the National Provisional Ruling Council soldiers (NPRC), the Revolutionary United Front rebels (RUF), the Sierra Leone Army (SLA) and God knows what.

These groups of people were all armed, all fighting each other and all living in one country, mostly in the same capital city. Jonny Paul and his government were subsequently removed. He was arrested or killed. Most of us still do not know what happened to him, his death or disappearance holds a lot of theories. Tejan Kabba was forcefully reinstated just as he predicted. He was reinstated with a lot of souls lost, a lot of souls gone and a lot of souls damaged.

We would sometimes sit on the balcony discussing how the bombing was killing people or how it had killed a lot of people and how it was affecting us the everyday people, how it was affecting our everyday life. We discussed how what they were doing was inhuman or not good or not right. We would have frequent, heated debates amongst ourselves. It was on one of those nights I saw an armoured tank, or tank, appearing in front of our house, it was coming down the street in almost a slow motion. It was pitch-black; we were using a lantern lamp. The generator was not on, or we may have just switched it off, the generator could not be left for too long due to fuel shortage and the price of fuel.

I heard something like a rumbling sound rolling not only on the street, but it was coming towards our direction. By now the place was completely silent. Am sure everyone of us was watching. Before I could make sense of what I was seeing, about seven to eight solders holding all kinds of weapons jumped out. They were in an aggressive or dramatic or soldierly manner. They barged through the gates and rushed up the few steps, their boots making a stomping sound as they approached us. No greetings or pleasantries as they started ordering us around. One of them was holding an RPG, the others an AK47 and other weapons but I didn't know what they were called. "Kneel down on the floor!" one of them shouted.

"Everyone kneel down!" another one repeated.

"Raise your hands up!" said another one.

I was still in confusion and in total disbelief, I just stood there unable to move and trying to take it all in or to process what was really taking place. Then one of the soldiers used his knee and kicked me on the buttock, the impact moved me forward a bit.

"I said kneel down and put your hands up," he shouted in a snappy tone.

I did as I was instructed, all the weapons were pointed at us very closely.

The ones who spoke to us were yelling in a Nigerian accent which was unmistakable. "Are you a collaborator?" No one said anything, so he continued talking, "We received intelligence about this house."

We told them we were definitely not collaborators. Mr Amadu spoke to them, he was the elder brother of our landlady. "We were just having a conversation in the night that is all."

Before he could finish, he interrupted. "No more open conversations, understand." he looked around and pointed at Mr Amadu, "You, come with us."

They took the landlady's elder brother with them. He was put in prison for about a week or two before he was released.

Fudia's health condition was worsening. We had seen almost every medical doctor in every hospital in Freetown. I was seriously filled with concerns. She had completely lost her hearing by now and she had lost a lot of weight. We could barely pay the rent. The money we had all went on food and on medication. The bombings and subsequent events which took place had shaken us all.

Mr Amadu moved out and stayed with other family members. Fudia went back to her mother and Baio moved in briefly with my mother before he went to university. There had been incidents when people who were accused of being a collaborator were killed or found dead or went missing. It was a known fact in the city.

The area where my mother lived in King Hamman Road had a lot of empty houses. The owners had fled and left their houses. The houses had been looted and no one was living in them. In some cases, only the caretaker or gate man lived in them. My mother told me she had spoken to one of the caretakers, I could take a room there for the time being.

Then she raised her hands up and started saying something about the solder who had kicked me. I just smiled and said, "At least we are still alive." I stayed there for a while and a little mormality or something that looked like normality started to return to the city. Baio got accepted at Fauray Bay college and I enrolled to the College of Business Studies in Wellington or Calaba Town. The location of the college was in between the two areas or close to each other.

The rebels were now very close to Freetown and they called themselves the west side boys. Others said it was not the rebels who resided at Okra Hill. They said it was the breakaway from the Sierra Leone army who were chased out by the Tejan Kabba government that resided at the Okra Hill and called themselves west side boys. I couldn't tell you for certain. Because I didn't know for certain.

And on 6 January 1999 the Revolutionary United Front commonly known as RUF entered Freetown. They came through the east end of the city, around the area where I used to live. What they did was impossible to comprehend and impossible to forget. They cut off people's limbs, killed them, raped civilians, some were burnt alive and most of the houses in Freetown were also burnt down. It was the things which you could not be expected to be see in real life.

It was something another human would not, or should not do to another human, something a Sierra Leonean would not do, or should have never done to a fellow Sierra Leonean. But they did, and they did it openly for everyone to see, without a care or any fear of anyone or any consciences.

It was a brazen attack on humanity. It was a needless war; it could have been prevented or avoided. We still don't know for certain the reason for the war. Because most of the reasons which they gave for starting the war or for fighting the war make no sense to me. The same reasons are happening today, if not worse.

The government eventually negotiated with the rebels and they formed a coalition government. then finally some peace or what looked like peace was restored. Some sanity and normality slowly crept in.

Some of the British army who were held hostage by the west side boys were also rescued by the UK government.

Chapter 16

Every day around the same time and at the same spot, I would wait for transportation to go to college. The commute was at least two hours to go and two hours to return on a good day. Some days just getting through PZ, Eastern police and guard street could take over an hour. I started noticing a man in a 4x4 who would slow down by the roadside, sometimes he would even stop for a few moments, and each time that happened, I would just act like I had not seen him or I would pretend to not notice him and look the other way. Then one day the car pulled up right next to me and stopped. A familiar voice called my name, I stepped forward to check who it was and it was Mr Salisu.

He was one of our teachers at the College of Business Studies. He was working with the United Nations Mission in Sierra Leone called UNAMSIL and was also teaching part-time in college. "Come in Christiana, am going to college." I climbed in and said thank you. After I sat down, I greeted the man in the driving seat. He turned around looking directly at me as he spoke, "Mr Salisu, so you know this woman."

"Yes, she is one of my students at college," he responded.

"Do you know I have tried to give her a lift so many times and she kept acting like I was invisible?"

I smiled and looked out of the window. Then Mr Salisu said, "Well maybe her mother warned her not to get into the car of a stranger." The three of us burst out laughing.

When we got to the college Mr Salisu got out of the car first and I got down and thanked both of them. Just as I was about to go, he got out of the car and said, "Hi, my name is BB, I would like for us not to be strangers, I don't want to be invisible to you anymore." I smiled a small smile. "I pass you on the road almost every day." I could not stop myself from smiling at this point. "Here is my card. Call me or I will start attending this college too." Well, what other choice was there, especially when he put it like that, I thought to myself. He held my gaze as he handed the card to me. I introduced myself, we both smiled, he noddenod and I walked up to college.

It was on a Friday that I went to spend time with Fudia, just one of the regular visits. We had gone from one church to the next, and hospital to hospital to hospital. She was not the same anymore. Communication was becoming a guessing thing. She would have to try to read your lips so she could understand what someone was saying. And I would have to sound the words in a way for her to understand with the movement of the lips. Every time I left her, I felt completely helpless and guilty for leaving her. When I got back to my place and brought out my books to do some coursework, a card fell out. I picked it up and smiled.

It was a Sunday evening when I dialled the number. "Madam are you ok? I was beginning to think you would never call." A small smile then I answered, "Am fine, how are you?"

"Let me come and pick you up so we can talk properly, then I can tell you how am doing."

I thought about it before I spoke, "That might not be a good idea right now, am just about to do some homework."

"It will not take too much of your time, there is a place by the beach, just a few minutes, let's just have a talk." Hmm, someone is being assertive, I said to myself. By the time my clothes were changed, he was parked in front of the house by the roadside where I normally waited for a taxi. We chatted over some pepper soup, we talked about almost everything, from families, to politics, to religion and relationships. We spoke briefly about my father and he told me how he had just lost his wife to cancer a few years back.

He said he was finding it difficult especially not living with his children anymore. I just listened as we walked. "You see that did not take long, did it?" he asked just as we sat in the car. Looking at me he said, "I thought you didn't talk much when I first saw you."

"What made you think that?" Now I was looking at him.

"Well, you know," he moved his head from side to side as if trying to find his reasons, "you just don't look like someone who talks so much."

"Oh, what does an individual who talks so much look like?" I answered.

"I just know what they look like and you are a talker who does not look like a talker." I was still looking at him as he explained.

"Am an expert in figuring people out." he went on.

With a smile I said, "Really, what else are you an expert on?" "Just wait, you will soon find out." He laughed some kind of boyish laugh. He dropped me back to the house. "It was good talking to you madam."

"It was good talking to you too Mr BB." And with that he drove off.

BB and I had been seeing each other for a couple of weeks. He had never entered where I lived, and one day he insisted on coming inside my place. He kept passing by the bathroom. "Are you ok?"

He stopped passing and said, "No actually, am not."

"What is wrong?" I asked again.

"My God madam, you cannot live here, you cannot live like this."

I gave a little sigh of relief. I had thought that I may have said something to make his mood change so drastically. "I have lived here almost a year; the area is ok."

"That is not true, there is no main door in the house, look at this window." He shook the window which almost fell off. The door to my room was just held together by a few nails or something.

"These houses were vandalised, robbed, looted or bombed," I simply responded.

"Why did you not tell me? Am not leaving you here, come and live with me." He got out of the window and stepped close to me. "How will I be able to sleep after seeing this?"

That made me laugh. "You are over reacting." Then I sat on the bed and spoke, "Am not going to live with you, calm down."

"Am not calming down madam, this is a hazard waiting to happen. Anyone can walk in here and harm you."

"Am not moving in with you," I repeated. What would my church friends say? I thought. "Seriously am fine." What I was really thinking was what if moving in with him did not work out then what next?

"I have to go, am traveling to Bo first thing in the morning. You can do your homework in the garden of the thatched house." He knew I liked spending time there. He removed a key from a bunch of keys he was holding and pointed it at me.

"Hey, that is bribery Mr BB are you aware of that?"

"Well, am aware, but I will take my chances." He was still looking and pointing the key at me. I took the key from him and nodded slightly.

"When are you coming back?" I asked him.

"In two days," he answered.

"Have a safe trip Mr BB."

And then he was gone. I did not go to his place until he called from Bo, saying he would be returning to Freetown that evening.

Mohamed his cook helped me prepare some food for his return. He liked the greens with vegetable oil which I cooked from time to time. He came back around 7 pm to 8 pm and we both sat and ate at the dinner table.

Just as we were about to finish our meal, there was a knock on the door. Mohamed opened it, and a woman with a lot of hair extensions walked as if she was the owner of the house. She had gold jewellery on her neck and wrist, with her breasts pushed up together tightly. She was holding her mobile phone loosely and had what looked like a walkie-talkie. It was actually a walkie-talkie. I could tell from the way she was messing with it, she wanted me or whoever was around to see it.

She only spoke to BB, "I checked in the office, and they told me you were coming back today, so I decided to pass by." Then she looked me up and down as if to say you are no match for me.

"I've just returned back, as you can see," he responded and took the plate he was eating into the kitchen. His body language had changed drastically, mixed with annoyance and embracement. To put him out of his misery I got up and said, "I have to go, got schoolwork to complete."

He grabbed the keys on the table and said, "Let me drop you." By now, I was walking towards the door and said calmly, "You don't have to, I will get a taxi." Both of us were coming down the stairs at that point, me heading to the gate, him heading to his car. "Madam can you wait? Please just get in the car."

He was holding the door and pointing for me to get in.

"Hmm, how come you did not tell me about your girlfriend?" I asked as he drove.

"Can you just let me explain?"

"Yes, feel free to explain, the floor is yours." I was doing everything not to smile or laugh at the way he was unsettled.

"I met her when I started working at the office."

"En, hen," I said.

"We ended it a few weeks ago. Am actually surprised to see her in the house tonight, I have not spoken to her or seen her in days." He looked out of the window and looked back at me.

"Maybe it was only you who ended it on your part, did you sign some document to say this thing between us has come to an end?" He laughed, I looked at him and shook my head.

"Please let's not talk about this tonight madam, am really tired and don't know what to say to your non-stop questions." The way he said it and the flicker of guilt in his face just made me laugh even more.

"Where are we going?" I asked him as he took a different route to my house. He looked at me and carried on driving. A few minutes later he was driving by the beach. We ended up having a drink at one of the restaurants. He took me back after a few drinks and a long chat.

That was my first encounter with Kumba. After church one day, Baby-rose was narrating to me what her sister had told her about an event that had taken place in BB's house. When she had finished, I said, "That was not how it really happened but pretty close."

"Oh my God, Christiana, it was you, now it makes sense, all the absences from church." She was rubbing her hand and stamping one foot on the floor, with a huge smile plastered all over her face.

"Du ya mama put me don, tok you yone en lef me yone ya."

And she was laughing her head off. "Ok, tell me what happened or how it happened."

Which I did. There was a lot of back and forth which flowed from sister to sister after that. Baby-rose was one of my best friends in church, and Kumba was also best friends with Baby-rose's sister. What a coincidence. The sister of baby-rose and Kumba did not attend our church. I had never met them before all the drama which took place.

Every time BB picked me up, he would look behind me or by my side. Then he would say, "Madam I think you have forgotten something."

"Like what?"

"Like your bags."

"Are you ever going to give up on that matter?"

"As a matter of fact I will not," he responded.

"Let's make a deal."

"Go on, am listening."

"What if you stay in my place, then you can start looking for a place of your own. This place is really not safe."

"That sounds good when you put it like that."

"Does that mean you are doing it? Do we have a deal?"

"No, I just said it sounds good." I smiled and looked out of the window.

He made a frustrated sound, then, with a fresh wave of determination and enthusiasm, he said, "Look here madam, I spend most of my time working outside of the city, the house is empty most of the time, you will be doing me a favour to keep an eye on it." I said nothing.

The next time he picked me up I was holding extra bags. I waved them at him, and he got out of the car or jumped out of the car and took some of the bags from me. "Wow! Madam what made you change your mind?" Both of us were smiling from ear to ear.

"Well, Juba Hill is much closer to my aunt, Fudia and my grandmother's place. I can walk from Juba to Barbadoro on a fine day." I paused and looked at him. "Plus, the hut is another reason, and a certain Mr BB will not give the matter a rest."

I pointed at the road as if to say keep your eyes on the road because he kept looking at me. "This calls for a celebration madam, let's go before you change your mind." And he laughed while I was trying not to laugh, which never worked. That night he took me to a restaurant I did not even know existed in that city.

I spent more time with Fudia and the rest of the family. I visited them every day or every other day.

After a few months, the agent showed us two houses. One had three bedrooms and the other a single room. BB wanted me to take the three-bed house. Then I heard my father's voice saying, "Cut your coat according to your size." I opted for the single room. It was in Wilberforce again, but this time it was close to the market. One of my best friends Abie lived closed by, just a few houses between us.

Whenever BB was in town, I would spend time with him. It was on one of those days that he said to me, "I notice you don't scream during intercourse."

There was a silence. "Oh I had no idea I should be screaming."

"Not scream exactly, you know what I mean, you should relax and you should scream involuntarily. I don't think you are reaching climax."

There was silence because I knew what he was talking about. My other friend Abie from college was telling me one day that her husband had to put a hand on her mouth for her screaming to not wake the children up.

So, he basically talked me through it and he kept telling me to stop thinking about everything right now and relax. I finally did concentrate, and my body did what I had no idea it was capable of doing. It was like the ground shook from underneath my feet and my whole body was having an earthquake. I did not scream though, but I could see why people could scream or why they screamed. All I said after everything was, "Hmmm, expertise in that category too?"

He stroked my head and removed some hair from my face and said, "Well madam, you tell me?"

It was a holiday at the university and Baio and BB spent a lot of time together. They got on really well. He had met my aunt, my mother and some of the cousins. Everything concerning our relationship was going well.

Fudia's health was the only thing that kept me awake at night. Just out of nowhere one evening, he said to me, "I would like to go and meet your parents."

"You have met most of my parents What are you talking about?" I answered him.

"Am talking about meeting them formally, a formal introduction."

After some thoughts I said to him, "My sister is not well, that is really thoughtful of you, but there will be no formalities."

To which he responded, "She will get better some day, she will." And the conversation changed.

The following day in the bedroom, he rolled over looking at me and brought something out of his pocket. He took my hand and put a ring on one of my fingers. "Do you like it?"

"How can you ask me that, what is not to like Mr BB, how do you even know my size? It fits just right, thank you." Then I looked up at him. "You keep buying me stuff unexpectedly, why?"

"Because I want to madam." Then he was smiling, a pleased with himself smile.

It looked like one of those rings, no it couldn't be, he was not on his knees like I had seen it done ceremoniously. I quickly put that idea at the back of my mind.

I went to Abie's so we could watch a movie together, she was the master of renting good movies, her elder sister was there too. Just as I was about to sit down her sister said to me, "Did BB gave you that ring?"

"Yes, how do you know?" I answered.

"I know because that is an engagement ring. You are now engaged to him. This is how these western men do their engagement."

"Well, he never asked me, can I be engaged, it is just a ring?" I responded.

"No, it is not just a ring. Congratulations!" she added.

"Don't be dramatic," I said then we laughed, and she said, "You children nowadays, you should be celebrating." But celebrating was the last thing on my mind.

"Let me see." Abie held my hand and took a closer look. "Christiana, that is a very expensive ring."

"Sure." I put my hand down and said, "Jewellery is always expensive."

"No, you don't understand, I mean really expensive." Abie was the expert and lover of jewellery. She was the one who introduced me to Alice Jewellery, one of the biggest jewellery shops in town at that time. That was the reason my mother called her Abie bonghor, meaning "Abie gold"; she liked to put on a lot of gold jewellery. The other Abie from college she referred to as Abie school.

When we had a college break, he asked me where I usually went on holiday. "To my mother's or grandmother's, an aunt's, just to visit family members," I explained. "Now my mother, grandmother, and most of the family members are in the city, there is nowhere for me to go holidaying."

"You have never left the country?" he asked with a surprised face.

"I have actually. I have been to Conakry," I responded proudly.

"Am going to Abidjan then Lagos and Abuja. I would like you to come with me." I agreed, told Baio and Fudia, then we left.

In the Ivory Coast, the restaurants were huge and the menu looked a lot like art work. I ordered something that looked confusing and complicated to me, and when they brought the order, I picked up the menu, placed it side by side to what I had ordered. "You only ordered that, to prove a point didn't you," he said to me.

"Am I that obvious?" And we laughed as we ate.

In Lagos we stayed in Victoria Island, in Abuja we stayed in Sheraton and in Conakry we stayed at the Mariador Palace, then we came back to Freetown.

He was always travelling and each time he travelled he would bring me stuff. One time he brought me lots of clothes and when I saw the prices on some of the clothes, I said openly, "Who spends that amount of money on clothes?"

"Me, and you are going to wear them."

Still looking at the clothes I said, "Why would anyone spend that kind of money on clothes?" I was having a mini tantrum all of a sudden. "And why are you always buying me stuff?"

"Because madam, if I didn't, you would never ask," he responded calmly and simply.

"Is it not supposed to be the other way around, ask and you shall receive?"

"Hmm noted, but for now please just put one of them on and let's go out, ok." I was still standing by the window looking over the hut at the backyard and holding one of the dresses. "Hey," then he put his hand around my shoulders, "what's wrong, don't you like your clothes?"

"I like them, it's just that I cannot buy you anything back, not now anyway."

"Madam, is it not, ask and you shall receive?" I turned to look at him. "Wait until I ask you to buy me clothes before you can begin to worry about that, ok."

"Very funny, touché Mr BB." And we were laughing again. "How can I thank you?"

"By putting one of them on so we can go out, and by continuing to be you."

"Be me, what is that?"

"You don't know?"

"No I don't." He grabbed me and gently threw me on the bed. "Ok madam, allow me to show you."

"I thought we were going out Mr BB?"

"Going out can wait, this cannot."

"Do you ever stop asking questions?"

"Yes, only when you are showing me like this."

"I see, from now on I will be showing you often."

After he had showed me, I showered and put on one of the dresses and noticed how different I was looking. I had gained some weight and I liked it. I was also feeling different, feeling more like a woman; my chest and bum had increased, the straight cut or flat waist they usually called me was now changing. They would now call me curvy.

On his birthday, I bought him a traditional item of clothing. In my place, most individuals would put on their Africana, as we called it, to go out. He was standing in the living room waiting for me so we could go out. "You are wearing that again?" I asked him.

He looked past me with such effect, I had to turn around to see what he was looking at. "What?" I asked.

"Am just looking for the palaver you brought with you downstairs. Are they not my clothes? I can wear them as many times as I want. Can we just go in peace please?" He walked out of the living room and I followed him.

Whenever I was in church, friends would ask me where I got my clothes from, and I would just say, "A friend bought them for me."

"Which friend, you mean your boyfriend?" Sia was giving me a grilling one day. All I did was cover my mouth as I laughed at the fact that she had got it so right. No admissions or denials were made, I just tried to move the conversation in another direction, by asking, "What was the reason behind you girls asking me or wanting me to be your bridesmaid?" I liked my friends, and I liked the fact that they were getting married, but I didn't like weddings. Or maybe it was the preparations and stress which came with it that I didn't like. Either way, I was not one of those women who fantasised or dreamt about getting married. The only part I liked at a wedding ceremony was the part when the bride and groom kissed. So, we could go onto the eating, drinking and dancing part, which for me was always the best part.

I was made a bridesmaid about three or four times in one year or in between two years. When BB picked me up from one of those weddings one night he spoke, "I want the children to come to Freetown when they have their break from school."

"No problem, I will be at my place when they come, don't worry about it."

"Madam the point is for you to get to know each other, not for you to vanish into space or to your own place." I laughed a worried laugh, and started thinking, what if his children didn't like me, or if we didn't get along or if the death of their mother was still too fresh to them to see their father with someone else? As if he knew what I was thinking he looked at me and said, "It is fine, you will be fine, trust me."

When they, two girls and a boy, came from Vienna, they liked it in Freetown and decided to come back and attend school there. It was on one of those holidays that he asked us in the living room where we wanted to go for a holiday. As they were looking around, discussing amongst themselves, trying to decide, I said, "Don't look at me, I have no idea, you just choose. I might come or I might not come with you."

They decided to visit England because their elder sister had just had a child. Ah, England, now I was definitely not coming, I thought to myself. He casually said to me when we were alone, "You can go with them."

And I answered, "How? Am not going with them, I don't have a visa to go to England." I had a friend Salomi, whose mother lived in the UK, and she was refused a visa about three times. I knew getting a visa was difficult. So many of my friends had been in similar situations.

"Hmmm," he said as he scratched his head and squinted on one side of his face. "Give me your passport and we can all apply for the visa together. I have to go for a meeting in the UK when you guys return."

We got the passport and he sent them to the British Embassy. I can't remember if it took a few days or a few weeks, I don't know how long it took. I was not paying attention to it. And I told no one about it. All I know is, I was having a nap, it was a hot afternoon, the air conditioning must have been on because I did not hear the car drive in. All I remember was a tap on the arm and he said, "Madam, here is your passport. We've all got a visa for England." I was stunned. That woke me up and sat me up.

"How did you do that?" I asked him while looking at the visa.

"You don't really know the kind of work I do, do you?" "Apparently not," I responded, still looking at the visa, "but getting a UK visa this quick is a very good job Mr BB." Now I looked at him with a surprised and a very sweet smile. The "ha, eureka! or got you!" smile reappeared on his face.

"Very impressive indeed," I told him.

He called his children and they booked a bed and breakfast in Camden Town, walking distance to where their elder sister was staying.

When we arrived in England, I was shocked, it was not what I had in mind or how I had envisioned it to be. I was expecting individuals to be dressed like the queen or as members of the royal family.

What I was greeted with were a lot of piercings all over their bodies and faces, plenty of dark clothes and a lot tattoos, the hair was big and vibrant. I was really taken aback. I had expected them to dress in suits, all slick and all talking and looking somehow different to what I was seeing. Well, that was what I got and what I was greeted with.

For breakfast, the full English one was also expecting to feast on was not in sight. It was toast, butter, jam, tea and coffee. The rooms were so small.

With the initial expectation about the UK being wrecked, I quickly recovered and began to relax by taking it all in. I even got in on the act and got my second ear pierced in Camden Town, one of the children got a belly button piercing, the other got something else. The three of us did something on that day. We visited their elder sister, we walked there, spent some time with her then returned back to the B&B. After that I called some friends and family. One of them took me clubbing to Equinox or something, it was around Trafalgar Square. The lights, the people, the place was jam packed, the music was fast paced. I think I enjoyed it a little bit.

Some days the children and I would spend it together and other days they would spend it with their sister while I went visiting. Aunty Saudatu took me to the shops where she usually did her own shopping. I bought a few items for myself. Then I told her I didn't want to spend all the money on myself, I was going to buy some clothing stock so I could start selling again. She took me to Finsbury Park. I bought a lot of things. I knew what the girls liked to wear in church, I also knew what they liked to wear in the nightclubs. But there was a problem. What was I to do with the excess I was accumulating? With three other suitcases from the children, we could distribute it amongst us, and we did.

When we returned, I went to see my aunt with Fudia. Then the following day when BB was at work, I called everyone I knew who would want to buy clothes. BB was speechless when he saw me busy negotiating and selling in his living room. He had had no inkling of what was going on. The "pocket money" he gave to us, as he put it, I had used it to start my own little business again. I made extra pounds. When I showed him the pocket money and the profits I had made, all he said was, "You like doing this kind of business?" Nodding shyly and smiling shyly was my response. I gave him the money so he could keep it or hold it for me for whenever it was needed. He doubled it when I asked him for it later on. I had more than what I had started with, and I still had a visa.

I went to England alone this time, bought everything, then shipped the items to Freetown. By the time they would arrive in about six weeks' time, it would be the Christmas season. I stayed with Aunty Saudatu, her husband and their son. The husband, Uncle Taworo, picked me up from the airport. I had known Uncle Taworo and most of his family members from Bumbuna. And his wife was from Magburaka. He worked full-time as a manager in Morrisons or something. While Saudatu was part-time at Marks and Spencer. The days when Saudatu was not working, she would take me around to more shops. We came back from shopping one evening when the phone rang. Aunty Saudatu picked it up, she said, "I will not be able to make it Babylee, I have promised to go shopping with Christiana on that day."

"I know a Babylee from Matotoka." The words came crashing out. Aunty Saudatu turned to me and asked, "Did your mother used to work as the nurse in Matotoka?" I nodded. "Are you Mormi?"

I said, "Yes. Is Babylee, Ya-mariam fullah's granddaughter?"

She nodded and said, "I think you know each other."

Aunty Saudatu passed the phone to me. "Mormi, how is Cisi Agnes?"

"She is doing fine, good evening, Babylee."

"Hey, you na big woman now en, you dae cam London for cam buy makit." I smiled. She had not changed I thought. Before I could get a word in, she continued. "Your husband is here; he is now living in Manchester."

"What husband?" I asked.

"Stop it, Amadu of course."

My heart did something. I was not expecting to talk of him or hear his name. "He is not my husband," I said weakly.

"Stop acting up, here take this number, call him before you go, ok."

"Call him for what?" I asked her.

"I don't know, just call him please, he is your husband." "Babylee, he is not my husband." We both laughed over the phone as I wrote the number down.

"Before you go back to Freetown, please let's see each other, it has been a long time. I called to invite Saudatu, if you finish with the shipment early, to come to the house for a little get-together for my mother, and I want to see how big you have grown now." Babylee and Amadu were first cousins.

At the Robert Clear shipment, because we went as early as we could, the shipping was done quickly. No more underground trains from one side of London to the other side.

Just before we left Robert Clear, a woman greeted me, "How are you, Christiana?" I searched her face, she looked really familiar. She said, "Don't you remember me? I went through the Bondo society with you."

"Yes, I remember very well now. How are you and how is your elder sister?"

"We are all fine. She will not believe me when I tell her I saw you, wow you have grown big and tall." We both laughed, chatted for a few minutes and we left.

On the way Aunty Saudatu said, "Well I think we have time for the Babylee invite since we have finished so early." We went to the get-together later on that day and I saw Babylee and her mother, her sister Ramatulie and a lot of people I had not seen for a long time.

"Have you called Amadu?" Babylee asked.

"No, I have not."

"Please stop being stubborn Mormi, just call him, ok."

"I will call him later," I responded and got a drink. What would I say to him? Would he even remember me? So many years had passed, what if he was married? His younger sister Lamrana told me he now had a son and I saw the pictures of his child.

The next day when Taworo and Saudatu left for work and Junior their son was in school, it was only me in the house. After deliberating with myself. I went outside for a long walk. On the way back I noticed a payphone and before I could stop myself, I was putting coins into it and dialling the number. A voice came at me on the second ring, it said the hello slowly. "Amadu, its Christiana, what Christiana? Is it Mormi?" There was a brief silence which seemed so long. "Mormi, is that you?"

"Yes, it is me."

"My God how are you? I have been thinking about you a lot."

I laughed a "yeah, whatever laugh". "You have been here how many years now, about eight, nine, ten, how come you never contacted me?"

"I did, I asked my brother Alie about you every time, but he said he could not locate you." I took deep breaths trying not to interrupt him. "He told me everyone was scattered about since the war. I swear on my life."

"Well, I see Alie from time to time, sometimes I even visit your mom."

"Ok, come to Manchester so we can talk more."

"Why would I want to do that, you want your wife to kill me, I saw the pictures of your son?"

"No am not married. I had a baby and we moved on, am going to Freetown in the next few days, I have to sort some business out and I have not seen my mother since I left."

"Oh, I see, that is the reason you have been thinking about me lately," I spoke with a little bit of annoyance.

"Don't be stupid, I have never stopped thinking about you. Are you planning on staying in the UK? You can come to Manchester when I come back. Am only going for about ten to twelve days."

"No am not staying, am going back to Freetown in less than a week's time. I have finished what I came for, but I have to wait for the return date on the ticket. Safe journey, who knows I might bump into you when I get to Freetown if you will still be around?" "Stop playing woman, take my brother's number and call me when you get back to Freetown, I really want to see you."

Babylee called in the evening, with laughter in her voice. "I thought you said you were not going to call. Amadu called to tell me you too spoke."

"We just talked Babylee, it is nothing."

"Yeah, if you say so, call me before you go and don't forget to call your husband when you get to Freetown." We said our byes and she hung up.

Chapter 17

I came back to Freetown with exciting and conflicting thoughts.BB must have noticed something was amiss because he kept asking me if I was ok. I told him I was fine, and had been thinking about what he said about not wanting more children which was to be a focal point to any decision making.

"Am not sure I want to go through life without having children." And he said, "I sincerely don't want any more children, I just turned fifty with five children. You are still in your early twenties, there is no way I would stop you from having children of your own if you really want them." He paused and carried on. "Those little rascals enter your life and change everything."

"My God, when you put it like that one can almost want to change their mind about them," I said shaking my head and smiling. We both laughed an understanding laughter.

"Seriously, if you meet someone who deserves you, and if you want to start your own family, just let me know. I will never stand in your way."

"Deserves me? What do you mean by that?"

"Well madam, you will find out one day, you will see, it is what has been eating you up. Don't worry about it, life has a way of sorting itself out." With that the conversation quickly changed again to the business.

I called my friend Isata, who owned a small clothing shop, and some of the other people who had boutiques in town. They would buy in bulk prices or I would give them credit then collect the money at a later date. When the things arrived, my friend Salomi brought two of her own friends to buy or take and pay later. And within two days the stock had been distributed.

After Salomi's friends left, we got talking, "Sister, wait, wait, slow down, which Amadu are we talking about? You mean Amadu, the Amadu." I nodded vigorously, smiling like a three-year-old child. "And you are here, saying you don't think you are going to see him, me sister, please don't do that, you will regret it, you have to sit down and talk to him," she said firmly not smiling.

"Geees, ok sister, I will, take am easy." We both smiled.

"You better do, or you will never forgive yourself." I escorted her to go and get a taxi. Then I finally plucked up the courage to call his brother's number. It was Amadu who picked up the phone. "Mormi, I was getting worried, you came back two days ago, and you did not call."

"Was just trying to sort business out."

"Am sending my sister with the driver to pick you up, just give them the address." He passed the phone to his sister.

A few minutes later his sister Porseh told me they were waiting at the junction. I still had the hair extensions from the trip, nails nicely done in London and was wearing a T-shirt, pale blue jeans skirt, knee-length with a small slit in front, and blue Nike trainers. A bit of make-up and I was ready to go. It was one of them very hot days.

By the time the car pulled up to his place, my palms were getting a bit misty, and my throat was getting dry. I didn't want to go and see him yet I really wanted to see him. Dilemma, you are a difficult thing.

The car pulled over at his mother's house in god-rich. He was waiting outside. I saw this man with braids open the car, take me by the hand, look me up and down then smile. Wish I could tell you what that smile was. Then he exclaimed, "Wow! You look good, Mormi."

"Don't call me Mormi, no one calls me that anymore."

"Ok Christiana, you have really looked after yourself."

"I did not, God did," I said in a whispered voice.

I wanted to say, you are looking fine too but thank God those words did not come out. Just by looking at him in the vest he was wearing, there was an indication of him hitting the gym. After greeting everyone including Alie, the brother who could not locate me, he took me to the end of the veranda. Then it was just the two of us.

We sat opposite each other face to face, just staring. "My God Salomi, am going to kill you," I was saying to myself. "You should have said no way, whatever you do, don't go and see him." Now I was sitting there, all words had failed me, I could not think, I could not talk, my hands were starting to tremble slightly. Even composure, oh composure, was not helping at this moment. He must have noticed; he excused himself and came back with some soft drinks. After a few sips, then composure and normal behaviour slowly started to resurface.

He finally broke the silence. "I heard about Fudia, am really sorry, how is she doing?"

"Some days good, some days not so good." Then we spoke about his child and the relation or relations leading to the child. And we spoke about BB.

"This BB, you like him huh?"

"Yes, I do like him a lot," I answered sincerely.

"Tell him to stay away from my girl."

"Really, where have you been all these years and am not your girl?"

"Well, am here now and he should stay away, or are go bos E bele." We laughed.

"No, you are not going to puncture his stomach, I will not let you do that." My words had returned.

"That old boy should really stay away from you."

"That old boy is really energetic."

"I will give you energy Miss, I will."

"No thanks, you can keep your energy."

"Nah you going to get it." Then we started teasing each other about events that had happened the last time when I visited my aunt. Or about events when we used to play at Matotoka. We laughed a little and I left.

The next day, I called Salomi. As soon as she picked up the phone she said, "Sister, I am already on my way to you, am coming for all the gist." She lived in Congo Cross at the time. When she arrived, she took one look at me and shook her head, with a smile that showed all her teeth. She said, "I think BB is in trouble."

"I don't know what you are talking about, we are fine," I answered her smiling too.

"Hmmm, tell me what did you and Amadu talk about? Are you going to see him again?"

"Maybe, something like that," I responded. "He said BB should back off now or he would kill him." And we laughed.

"Told you BB is in trouble."

The relationship with BB had not been the same since his children came to stay. They had lost their mother, I was young and BB found himself playing referee between us. He was travelling often, leaving me with the children. We started to argue about every silly thing. Sometimes I would even pack my things and go to my place and after a while, I would return not wanting to leave them on their own. I did see Amadu again before he left. He asked me to come to Manchester next time I was in England.

"I will think about it," I told him, which was the truth, I needed to weigh out the pros and cons.

One day after having dinner with BB I told him about Amadu. He looked at me and said, "I hope he is a good guy."

"I know his family and I have known him since we were children," I said to him, "I think he is."

"Well we can only pray he has not changed." he added. "People can change, especially when they have been in Europe for that long." he went on. The conversation was very frosty.

I was still going to the College of Business Studies (CBS) and Fudia was still not well. A recent visit to the hospital gave me cramps in my stomach and I was tearful all day. It was not looking good. They told us to prepare for the worst. I told them it could not be, they must have gotten the results mixed up or wrong. And I took her back to the house.

Mr BB's children decided to go to America for their elder brother's wedding, or something. After that they would go to university or college outside Sierra Leone. BB wanted them to study in Ghana or they wanted to study in Ghana. I told BB I would be going to England to buy more stuff for the business. I put some money in my Commercial Bank account. And I made sure Fudia had enough for medicines and food. I gave Baio all the names of people who owed me money.

Amadu and I had already hatched a plan. If I came back to England, I should stay with him permanently. He said, "Don't tell BB he might not let you come." I told him he was not like that. To which he said, "You don't know men; they might say they are fine, but when the time comes, they might not find it so easy and will act funny."

"How do you know all this, is it because you are a man?"

"You have to come back before your multiple-trip visa expires," he said bluntly.

The days leading upto my departure were troubling me. I knew full well what I was about to do, and I knew it would change my life forever. I also knew I might never see Fudia again. I felt terrible, dreadful, risky and adventurous all at once.

Amadu paid for the tickets this time. I told him, "Am not paying for you to see your girl and BB is certainly not paying for your girl, I wouldn't let that happen."

"Ok no problem woman, I will buy the tickets for my girl," and went on to say, "you too get mout." It was going to be a big risk and it was too uncomfortable for me.

It could work or it could backfire. Before I left, the majority of my jewellery was stolen including the ring BB gave me. With a few thousand dollars in my purse, I left Lungai airport with no intentions of returning back to Freetown, or returning back to BB.

I arrived in London then got another flight to Manchester. He was standing there with a jacket in his hand. After we greeted and hugged, he placed the jacket over me. "This jacket is way too thick for this time of the season," I told him.

"Well, you are coming from a hot country I don't want you to start shaking all over the place." I rolled my eyes at him and we laughed. "Come let's go, welcome to Manchester." We got in his car, an Audi, and we drove along Littleton Road and branched off to Kersal Way.

We pulled up to a not-so-crowded semi-detached house, it was neat with wood fencing all around. Inside, the house was also neatly furnished with a massive television, cream three- seater and two single-seaters, leather sofas, a dining space with a glass dining table and white chairs. The kitchen was a good space: very clean and tidy. I didn't think that the kitchen had been used in a long while. The dining room had a back-sliding doo,r which opened out to a fair sized, well looked after garden. "Well Chris, this is it, come let me show you the bedrooms."

One of the rooms had a massive built-in wardrobe with fancy lights, sliding doors, and a king-size bed, the other had a double bed, a television and a medium wardrobe. He said his brothers and friends stayed there when they came over. And the last room, which he called a box room, was very small, it had a computer table with a PC on top of it and some suitcases.

Then he showed me the bathroom. I had been travelling all day so I had a shower while he left to get us something to eat. When he came back, I was in the bedroom changing and trying to unpack. He came up to the bedroom and I said, "Come on man, can I rest first?"

"No you can rest later, come here."

"Easy up man, are you trying to kill me?" I must have screamed slightly. "You have to learn fast and get used to it." Gees how strong he is, what happened to that eighteen-year-old boy? I asked myself. As we were eating, he kept looking at me. "What?" I asked.

Smirkingly, he said, "Was that energetic enough for you?" "Shut up." Then I threw a little piece of food at him. After eating I went to the other room and watched television while he stayed in the living room playing on his Xbox or something.

When I woke up in the morning, he had gone to work. I called Aunty Saudatu and her husband. "You left BB?" she asked, her voice questioning and disapproving. "I hope Amadu is worth it." She did not sound pleased. The call with Saudatu did not last long. BB had been calling her house, checking and asking for me and she did not know what to tell him, which was true as Saudatu had no idea of my actions. I called BB and told him I was not coming back. He said, "I know Madam, I was not going to stand in your way. I gave you my word and I wanted you to make the decision and take a bold step all on your own." That made me cry. I could not speak, I was sobbing. After the silence he said, "Take care of yourself. If you ever need anything, call me." Then the line went dead.

I sat there thinking. My God, he caught this bird, mended its wings and he was letting it fly the nest, letting it back into the wild. Instead of keeping it in captivity, he was letting the bird use its wings instead of clipping them. How honourable was this man? He was no doubt "God sent".

I called Salomi, called my brother and broke the news to them. I was surprised that almost everyone had seen it coming. Our little secret was not so secret after all. I had breakfast and unpacked. What had I just done? I thought about Fudia, and wished she could hear, I would love to talk to her when I was in this kind of situation. She had always known how to calm my nerves. I prayed for her and felt guilty for leaving her. Amadu came back early evening and picked me up, he took me to a place in Moorside where he bought some curry goat with rice and peas.

"I get food from here sometimes," he said as he got out of the car. I stayed in the car while he picked up the food. He was definitely living a life of takeaways.

When he got in the car, I said to him, "I think that woman likes you," referring to the woman who was dishing out the food. "Shut up." He was looking at me as we both laughed. He was shaking his head. "You taking the piss at me en, just wait, I will get you soon," he answered, smiling and looking at me teasingly.

"Is that all you could think of?" I answered back.

"Yes, you are all I could think of, come on, it's been almost ten years."

"And whose fault is it?"

"Ok miss, let's not get into that right now, come let's go, am starving."

We ate dinner and went for a walk around the area where he showed me the gym which the residents had access to. It had a swimming pool and a tennis court. "Don't you cook anything?" I asked as he was showing me around.

"I don't know how to cook anything; you know me, I never went near the kitchen."

"Your grandmother tried teaching you how to cook or farm but you refused."

He laughed. "I certainly gave her the run around, I was so glad to see her again, she still remembers me," he explained.

"She remembers everyone. When I went to visit her one day, as soon as I entered her room, she said, 'Is this not the one they call Mormi, nurse Agnes's daughter.'"

Amadu laughed loudly and said, "That is her."

"I was flabbergasted, I had not seen her in over eighteen years."

"I don't know what they ate in those days, but their memory is really good," he said, and asked about my grandmother. I explained, "She still has all her teeth and all of her memory. The only thing is that her hands shake slightly and she is not very mobile like she used to be."

"I can't believe they are still alive, it's a miracle," Amadu said.

"Just before I left, my grandmother said in front of everyone that she was waiting for me to have a child before she could die. So, when she goes, at least she will have something to tell my father."

He smiled. "In that case, let's go and give Grandma a message to take to your father."

"No please, do not bring my grandmother into it." We entered the living room and sat on the sofa. We did not make it to the bedroom. Before I knew it, he was giving me more energy. My God is this what he meant by get used to it, I said to myself as I hurried to the bathroom.

Chapter 18

Amadu worked in an amusement arcade in Manchester. He was one of the managers. Most times he would leave the house very early in the morning and come back really late at night. I would spend the day going to the gym. Some days I would go for a long walk and other days I would just go for a bus ride. I would go to the Trafford Centre or the Arndale Centre sometimes.

I would clean the house and tidy the house. It had just been a few weeks but me indoors and a television all day was not something I was used to.

In my place, we didn't watch television. Most of the time, we were simply the television. We would spend the time with families, friends, churches, schools, farm, garden, beach, doing business, nightclubs, going for a run, you get the idea. It took a long time for me to adjust to spending the whole day by myself with not much to do. He introduced me to his friends Watson, a Jamaican, and Joseph from Sierra Leone. He also introduced me to Joyce the woman whom he said that if he ate Sierra Leone delicacies in Manchester, it would be from her. I also met Ebrahim and his girlfriend, Dee. Some weekends we would go clubbing in a place called Sugar-Lounge or Stock in a club called The-Place. Sometimes he took me shopping.

I told him I needed to do something, I wanted to go to the school of nursing. He found out about it and we went to enquire in the school. We explained ourselves. The woman took a look at my passport and said that with a visiting visa I was not allowed to study or work in the UK. We left and visited a legal firm's office to get some more advice on my situation. The lawyer told us that the law had been changed. To be able to work or study in the UK the best chance was to get married to a British citizen, then go back to Freetown. It was the British Embassy in Freetown who could decide to give me a resettlement visa.

The fairy tale had abruptly come to an end. Amadu looked at me when we got into the car and said, "Well, we have to get married and start the resettlement process or there is no use staying in the UK if you are unable to do anything." I was really upset; this was not what I had hoped for. I thought once I got to the UK, I would be able to arrange all the paperwork here. I was not expecting to have to go back to Freetown and start the paperwork all over again. What if Amadu met someone else and forgot about me while I was in Freetown? It's not like he hadn't done it before and blamed it on the war or his brother. We went to the registry office and booked a date for the wedding, we told Joyce and a few close friends and family members.

I went to a wedding shop and tried on the first wedding dress I picked; it was my size, it fitted, so I took it straight to the cashier and paid for it. The assistant said, "Don't you want to try on a few more dresses?"

"No, this one is ok, it's the right size, I like it." And I smiled. With a pair of bridal shoes to go with the dress, I paid and left the shop.

Fudia had died just a few weeks after I left, I was still mourning my sister. Being joyful about a wedding was the last thing on my mind. The day of the wedding, I woke up, did my own hair and make-up, dressed myself up and sat there feeling out of place. There was a knock on the door. When I went to answer it, it was the florist. Amadu had ordered the most beautiful bouquet of flowers I had ever held. The flowers lifted my spirits a little bit. They were beautiful, delicate, white roses wrapped in large green leaves. What a pleasant surprise. I could not put them down or stop looking at them. We went to the registry hall a bit early, another wedding was just finishing. Just as they called us in, he looked at me and said, "Well, you did not want to get married, now you have no choice but to get married." I did not even smile or say a word. The nerves had taken my words again. I just wanted it to be over before I ran out of the hall. After the I do, I relaxed a little bit. We went to Joyce's house where we ate, drank and danced before Amadu left for work. After Amadu left, we sat there chatting when Joyce, out of nowhere, asked me a strange question, "Christiana, how many children did Amadu tell you he had?"

I was confused by the question and timing; I was still wearing the wedding dress. I said, "What do you mean, he only has a son, and he spends the weekend with us from time to time?"

And she said, "Oh ok." Now I was thinking, how many children could there be? "How many children does he have?" I threw the question back at Joyce.

"If he only told you about one child, then he only has one child," Joyce answered back. She definitely was not being a total cow. There was definitely something to this question. She knew exactly what she was doing, she was not a child who could just ask questions out of curiosity. Hence it was my own wedding day, I was not going to ruin it any further by demanding or insisting on her elaborating on the subject. I kept quiet, besides I knew who to direct my questions to.

He finished up early on that day and picked me up from Joyce's place. I waited till we got home; I could no longer hold it in. So, I asked him the question as soon as we entered the house, "How many children do you have?" He was not expecting that question to just land on him like that. I was looking at him directly. I already knew he had more than one by the nature of the question.

All he said was, "I thought you knew."

"About what?"

"That I have two children."

"How could I have known?" He was looking uncomfortable. "I don't really see my other son; I have a lot of problems with his mother and the CSA is involved which just makes things really difficult."

The way he said it, I almost gave him a hug, but I did not, too pissed off to do that. "Well, I had no idea, you did not tell me, and I did not know until today when Joyce asked me a question. Are there any more children you might think I already know about?"

"Actually, there are no more children Mrs Sesay." I rolled my eyes, in a not friendly manner, we called it *bad-yie* in my place. I took the wedding dress off and went to bed, woke up very early in the morning, but just lay there. I could hear him getting dressed and leaving. I was pretending to be asleep. I still didn't want to talk to him at that point. I felt a shift in my life once more. I tried to put a hand on it but I could not.

As the weeks passed, we tried to get all the necessary papers needed for the resettlement application. The last weeks just zoomed by. We bought a ticket, and it was time for me to go back to Freetown.

Now I had no business or business money, the money I brought with me, I had given it all to Amadu for safekeeping. We had spent a lot of money organising the wedding since I came. It would not feel right to ask him for money. He had been paying for food and everything since I had arrived. "Stop worrying," he said to me and brought me back from my thoughts. "As soon as you arrive, go to the embassy, you will be back here with me, ok."

I nodded weekly. "We can only hope for the best," I responded.

"That's better, let's focus on a good outcome," he added.

It was one of the most painful goodbyes yet again. I arrived in Freetown really late, the ferry from Lungai to the city was delayed. There was always something causing a delay. We finally crossed to Freetown and I waited till morning before I visited my aunt.

The house felt empty without Fudia. My grandmother was crying when I sat by her. She said, "I prayed every day for God to take me instead of her, how can this have happened? An old woman stays alive and a child dies, where is the justice in that?" I just sat there feeling helpless, powerless and devoid from all zest of life. Pa Momoh, Fudia's father, took me to see her grave. I spent the next few days going from my bedroom to the bathroom, I could hardly eat. My appetite had gone. When I looked in the mirror, I saw how I felt, I saw the pain in my eyes, and the pain in my body. I did not tell people I was back because I wanted to be on my own. It was finally time to grieve properly for my sister. News quickly got around about my return. Some individuals were even speculating that maybe I had been deported. That was why I was always in the house or didn't want anyone to see me. I said nothing or did nothing to put them straight or to correct the false narratives. My mind was too preoccupied with relevant issues.

The morning of the interview I woke up, prayed and went to the embassy. We sat in a row in the corridor. They would call a person individually into a booth for the interview. I heard my name, went over to the counter and I was directed to the booth. The interviewer was a woman not too far from my age group. She must have been older than me by only a few years or so. She brought out the file and began the interview. She directed questions at me from every direction and every angle. She asked about my last visa, about Amadu's ex-wife, the one he had his first child with. "Do you know about her?"

I said, "Yes, I know about Brenda."

She asked me about BB and I explained about that. Then the interview was over. Very uncomfortable, besides it was a little easier when you were the one asking the questions. Now I had to wait for a decision to be made. I went back to my original seat and waited. The wait could not have been more than fifteen to thirty minutes but it felt like a very long time. Then it was time, I was called in again. "We have looked into your application for a resettlement visa. On the grounds of the relationships, I think the time you left one relationship and the time you got married was too short. So, on those grounds we are denying you a visa this time." My mind went blank. "You can re-apply after six months," she said, or something like that. Whatever she said after "deny", did not register, her lips were moving but I could not hear the words coming out of her mouth. It felt as though everything was moving backwards and in a slow motion.

By the time I came out of the gate the sun was already heating up. Clutching the file of papers, I walked all the way from the embassy to Wilberforce village, entered the bedroom, changed my clothes and went to bed. Amadu must be at work by now, I would tell him when he called in the evening.

I felt like karma was flogging me, then I was angry, how dare she judge me, telling me that leaving one relationship and getting into another one was too soon, my dear you have no idea I thought to myself. Everything was ok except the timing. Have you not heard about people getting married in a few days, after they have left one relationship? We got married months later, now I was having a palaver with her in my head.

When Amadu called it was almost night time and he must have known as soon as I picked up the call. I explained everything to him and in an exclaimed voice he said, "What!" A few moments passed before he spoke again, "We just have to get a lawyer involved then; we should have done it from the start." "Lawyer, no, that is going to be very expensive, I don't have any money on me for that," I said in a small voice.

"Don't you worry about that Or-Mrs, even if I have to sell this house, I will." He just called me Mrs again, I smiled a small smile to myself.

"The time will pass quickly, there will be a good outcome in the end, ok."

I said, "Ok."

"I have not eaten all day today, let me try and eat something," he continued.

"What are you going to eat? Is it from your you know what?" "My what?" he repeated the words from me with more emphasis.

"Your admirer. You know she likes you, that is why she always puts more food in your takeaway than mine." My voice was finally sounding like me again.

"Shut up you fool, you're lucky you are not near me. I should have put more on your plate right now."

"Honestly, don't you get tired?"

"Nope! I will speak to you tomorrow ok, love you, trouble." "Love you too." And he hung up. That conversation charged me up a bit, I felt like I was running out of power and now it was like I had been plugged in.

I sat there contemplating what I would have been doing by now if I had not had to come back, or if I was still with BB. You just can't stop your mind from wondering sometimes.

BB moved on soon after I left. I talked to Ami one of my friends who sold hair products on the main road where BB was now living. They moved from Juba Hill to a bigger house on Wilkinson Road. She told me she saw a woman in his car and later found out he was going out with that individual. She had two children from a previous relationship. "That was quick," I said laughing loudly.

"Ah look who is talking." She laughed. "Well maybe he found out you were manoeuvring to a different direction, so he made his own manoeuvre first." We laughed it off. Well, he really did not want any more children did he, I thought to myself. He called me weeks later and I explained the situation to him. He had seen someone who told him I was in town. "Don't worry, it will be fine madam." His voice was comforting as we ended the call.

There was not much for me to do now. Fudia had passed away, Baio was in Fourah Bay College (FBC), no more BB and his children, and there was nothing for me to buy or sell. I found myself spending a lot of time in church once more. I was there most of the time. I would stay after church to help and clean the church, scrubbing the floors just to pass the time. And sometimes I would go with my friend Fatu to the Lagonda nightclub. I would read books, sleep, spend time with friends, read the bible, go running on the beach or go for extra-long walks. I had gotten hooked on the *Harry Potter* series. One day I even took it to church. When brother Samuel saw it, he stopped right in front of me, looked at me strangely and said, "You should not be reading that kind of book sister Christiana, it is about witchcraft."

"Brother Samuel, that is exactly why I am reading it." I looked back at him. "Don't you want to know how they operate? I want to know what this witchcraft does, or what witchcraft is all about." He sighed and shook his head then walked on. Sometimes my friends would come to the house in the evening and we would cook Liberian *dry res*.

Liberian dry res was when you seasoned the fish with black and white pepper, added a maggi cube with lime juice. It was then fried in a way where the skin was crispy on the outside and the flesh was moist on the inside. Hot pepper was then fried in the same oil you used to fry the fish. You boiled the rice and ate it with the fish and pepper. It was that simple, straightforward and delicious.

Some days I would just spend with my grandmother. It was on one of those days when she told me she did not like living in the city anymore. She said she did not want to die in the city because the graves in the city were full; they usually buried individuals in old graves. More so, she wanted to be buried near her sons and their father. I said, "Granny, it looks like you are not the only one who wants to leave this city. Don't worry you are not dying just yet."

"Yes, Mormi, when are you going to give me something to tell your father when I die? All of your mates your age, your cousins around the same age as you, they all have two or more children, please even if it is just one, try and have a child."

"Don't worry Yah, soon ok, soon."

I sat there with not much to do and I was still feeling trapped. It was like my hands were free but my feet were chained. Amadu called me regularly to reassure me that the lawyer Aziz was on the case. He would also send me some money from time to time. We would talk about all sorts, from how we were missing each other, to family members, especially his mother whom I visited regularly.

Chapter 19

"Or-Mrs, am booking a ticket to The Gambia, I have a week's holiday, let's meet there, ok. We need to see each other Or-Mrs. It's been over three months. Go to the airline and see what date flights depart from Sierra Leone to The Gambia then let me know."

"Ok, Amadu."

Within a week I was with his younger sister, Haja and his friend Kabba on the ferry to the airport. I felt as light as a kite. When I saw him, I just flung my hands around him, and he held me tightly, too tight perhaps. He looked at me smiling and teasing as usual. "You don't look as bad as you sounded on the phone the other day." I smacked him lightly on the arm and laughed shyly. His friend in The Gambia had brought his girlfriend to pick us up and they were waiting with a taxi.

We stayed with them for the whole week. When we got into the house and put our bags down, their daughter, who was about two or three at the time, went to the room and just moved from Amadu to me, she refused to leave our sight. Any time Amadu tried to come near me the girl would come in between us. I could not stop laughing. He looked at me and said, "You are not going to hide behind the child for ever." We washed, changed and the four of us went out for dinner. It had been a while since I could relax again.

By the time we got back from dinner the little girl was asleep in her parents' room. Well, that which was waiting to happen, happened; the few days together brought us closer. We went out sightseeing, we visited the market, bird watching, we went to the beach and clubbing at a place called Jorkor. It was a memorable time.

By the time it could sink in, or I had got used to having him around, the week was over. It was time to say our goodbyes. "Try not to worry too much Mrs, Aziz said we have a good case."

We departed the same day; he returned to Manchester and me to Freetown.

The months passed by so slowly and there was nothing I could tell my grandmother every time I visited her. She was getting more adamant about going to the province. We finally agreed for her to go as she wished. Cici FA took her; she was going to stay with Uncle Sali and his wife. About a month or two after she left, Cici FA and I decided to pay her a surprise visit. As it turned out, it was us who got the surprise. We met her all by herself. Sali and the rest of the family had had to go to the farm. Because she could no longer walk long distances she spent most of the day by herself. My heart sank, I said, "Yah, you cannot live like this every day, you have to come with us, we promise you, you are going to be buried near your children, is that not so, Cici FA?" Cici FA nodded in agreement. "However difficult or expensive it is we will bring you back to Fadugu." Cici FA backed me up. The next day she was back in the city.

It was Just over a year since I had left Manchester. Amadu called to tell me that he would be in court with Aziz and the immigration officer regarding the resettlement visa. I felt the blood rush through my veins. I could not speak. "Don't stress," he reassured me, "I have all the documents they are asking for. We have a good chance. Our case is the first one to be called, it is not far from my workplace. I will just go to work afterwards."

"You are making it sound so straightforward. May God give his blessings," was the only thing I could manage to say.

"God has already given his blessings Or- Mrs." I could not say a word to anyone. I didn't want to jinx it.

I had an early night and woke up very early the next day, just thinking to myself, the "what ifs" kept flooding in. In fact, they had taken hold of me and my thoughts. I must have slept again because when I woke up it was almost 10 am. Amadu would have been in court by then.

There was only one hour difference between the UK and Sierra Leone. If I was not looking at the clock, I was looking at the phone. It was almost 4 pm, it must be bad news, that is why he has not phoned me. It was almost 8 pm when the phone rang. I ran to the bedroom and closed the door.

"Or-Mrs, the verdict went in our favour. Aziz, the lawyer, presented every evidence to support the case and he pulled it off, the immigration office will contact the embassy in Freetown, they will contact you, ok."

"Thank you," was all I could get out of my mouth. "God, thank you," I repeated.

"Sorry I did not tell you sooner, I have been rushed off my feet all day."

"Ok, no problem." I tried to jump up but I could not. I wanted to shout or run out of the house screaming. Please don't do that, my thoughts told me. Instead I just sat on the bed looking at the walls, then I lay on my back staring at the ceiling, the "what ifs" had evaporated and my nerves had calmed down.

I was not going to tell anyone until I was holding that visa in my passport. The day I got the visa in my hands, every step felt like the clamps had been removed from my feet. I felt the tranquillity within me reinstated, I was now looking forward to the new phase of my life, a renewed hope. Things were no longer moving backwards in slow motion, they appeared to be moving in the right path at the right pace, that was how every step felt. I was not going to tell a lot of people until I got to Manchester. I would only tell the closest family and friends.

I told my grandmother and my aunty, I told them not to tell anyone. I told Baio, Salomi, Ami and Abie. I told Isata my friend who always helped me to sell the clothes, she gave me a lot of dried fish and other food stock to take with me. I told Kabba, Amadu's friend, I told some of Amadu's family. Come to look at it, I told so many people.

I called Rugea, a sister friend: one of the girls from the mission, who was now working in the money exchange bureau at the airport. She always looked after me when I travelled. She knew the men and women who did the checking in, she would see to it that my bags were looked after and safe. Bags could go missing or misplaced sometimes.

It was just Kabba and Baio who came with me to the airport. Rugea was expecting us, the bags were checked in and we sat in her office until it was time to board the flight. She knew someone at the duty free. By the time we knew it, we were sipping on Disaronno and ordering food from the airport restaurant. Soon it was time to check in. Rugea had taught me not to say goodbye. I had had too many goodbyes come to think of it. When I stood at the door of the plane, I looked at the landscape for a brief moment, then I was in my seat.

I thought I might not see Manchester again. As I got off the train at Piccadilly Gardens station, Amadu took my bags as we grinned at each other without saying a word. We got into the car still grinning, and looking at me he said, "I took two days off, I told Paul Pierce you were coming, and he said I should take some time off." Paul was the general or regional manager.

"Thank you, Paul Pierce. If it was up to you alone, you would not have taken any time off." Both of us grinned again.

"Welcome back Or-Mrs." We drove off.

Within those two days, we visited Joyce Mustapha, we stopped by a house, and he introduced me to Lydia; she did his hair sometimes he told me. We saw Joseph, his friend, briefly and we went to the market to get some items. By the time we had finished it was almost night time. We got a takeaway from China Town. It was crispy duck, noodles, black beans sauce, with salt and pepper ribs. After dinner it was an early night for me, so I went to bed. A few moments later, he walked in. "Am having an early night too," he said as he got under the cover.

"What happened to your Xbox or PlayStation?" I asked. "Well I got a better game to play right now," he responded.

He was still sleeping when I got up and went straight to the kitchen. I was cooking cassava leaves when he walked into the kitchen, around noon. The palm oil from the cassava leaves was jumping from the pot and splashing everywhere from the cooker to the wall. "Why do you like cooking so much? Look at the mess you are making." He stood there watching, as I carried on mixing the plasas, which was still splashing on the wall. The expression on his face made me laugh.

"Please, I hope you have washed your mouth before rubbing it on me in the afternoon."

"I have washed my mouth actually, you cheeky woman." He went back to the living room and started playing on his Xbox. There was no breakfast. By the time we had lunch it was around 2 pm. "This thing is really good Or-Mrs, it is nice," he said with emphasis as he ate.

"What thing?" I said trying not to smile.

"The cassava leaves, it's been a long time since I ate some of it."

"Oh, so you don't like it been cooked in the kitchen, but you like it on the plate," I remarked.

"Don't be sarcastic woman." And he carried on eating.

I emptied the plates, put them in the sink then put the remaining cassava leaves in a plastic container and put it in the fridge. Now all the pots and plates were in the sink. As I was going upstairs to have a wash, he called after me. "Who is going to do all this washing up?"

"Not me." I tried not to laugh again.

When I came back downstairs, he was wiping the walls, and talking to himself.

"This is why I don't cook; it is too much work."

"No Mr, you don't cook because you don't know how to cook. You can't even boil an egg."

"Hey, I have warned you about your mouth, watch it."

"Well, why don't you come and watch it for me?" I was walking away as I said it. He grabbed me and we fell on the sofa.

"Get off me you animal, not now, not again. You should be tired with all that washing up."

"Am never tired, am only getting started, come here, this will shut your mouth."

"Get off," I said laughing.

"You talk too much, woman."

"You too fityie."

It was the last day before he returned back to work so we went to the school of nursing to enquire again. I still wanted to study nursing. They told me I could now study with that visa, but I would have to pay all the tuition fees by myself because I was not entitled to a student loan or any public funds. The fees were fifteen thousand pounds or more, a year or term. I was crushed. When we returned to the car, Amadu said, "That is a lot of money to raise with all the mortgage payments and bills."

"I know. There is still time. When I have all the required necessary documents, I will still do it."

"That is the spirit," he answered.

As usual he would go to work before I woke up. The weeks kept passing by. Once again there was not much to do. And when Amadu came back from work, we would only have a brief communication before I went to bed. We had picked up a lot of application forms which I spent most of the day filling out. Almost all of them kept asking for a year's or at least six months' experience. Very discouraging I thought to myself. I was walking along Bury New Road one day; I entered the McDonald's that was there and asked to speak to the manager. I spoke to him, and he gave me their forms. I told him I didn't have work experience in the UK. "Don't worry about, that we will train you, just fill out the forms and bring your passport with you." I returned the forms and passport the next day. Within a week I got a call with a start date for the training. I sat on the stairs facing the door, knowing Amadu would walk in at any time. I was grinning from one ear to the other. "I got a job," I announced.

"You did, where?" he asked.

"McDonald's," I told him.

"McDonald's," he repeated not so impressed.

"Yes, it is a start, everywhere else kept asking me for work experience."

"Congrats Or-Mrs."

Chapter 20

My job at McDonald's was to organise the parties held there for children, wipe the tables, mop the floor, clean the toilets, empty the bins and deliver food to the waiting customers, especially those waiting in the car park. Salford was known for its troublemaking teenagers. They would come in the evening and fight amongst themselves, pick a fight with the staff or just pour milkshake all over the windows and floors. Apart from that, it went well. It was not fixed hours. Some days I would start at 6 am to 3 pm in the afternoon and some days it would be 9 am to 11 pm. I worked about four to five days depending on the rota. There were two of us working in our department.

Six months had passed and still no message for my grandmother to take. I suggested we go and see a doctor. If there was a reason why I was still not pregnant, they might be able to tell us. He was reluctant but we went anyway. They took a blood test, urine samples, scans, swabs, and they gave Amadu a little container and asked him for a sperm sample. He kept on saying, "I can't do it, how am I going to get this out?" He was holding the tub in one hand and looking at me while he waved the tub. "Just get it out how you normally get it out."

"It is not that easy; you have to come in with me." Now he was looking worried.

"Just behave yourself, this is a hospital, remember that." And we both laughed embarrassingly. He finally managed to get some out.

When we came back for the result, he was told his sperm count and his sperm cells were healthy.

Obviously, he already had two children. It must be me, I said to myself.

The gynaecologist told me they had found fibroids in my womb. They should not stop you from conceiving because they are not blocking anything. "Can they be removed?" I asked.

"Yes, but there is a very high chance that your womb might be scratched and that can affect your chances of getting pregnant. Apart from that, I don't see any reason why you should not get pregnant." She looked at her notes and looked back up at me. "Your eggs are fine, and you are still in your twenties." The doctor told us, "I will put your name down on the list to start fertility treatments if you want me to, but I am sure you will be like a lot of the women who get pregnant while they are still on the waiting list to get treatments."

"Yes, put my name down, please."

"Try not to worry too much, reduce your stress levels and eat a balanced diet. Call me when you get pregnant, so I can take your name off the list and give the place to someone else."

"Thank you, doctor."

When Amadu was working, I would be sleeping. When he was sleeping, I was at work. Some days we didn't even see each other. Some days a brief conversation here and there and then he was on the Xbox playing while I watched the soaps. He still wanted me to go out clubbing with him. But after a long day's work, I would rather sleep, especially if I had to start at 6 am the next day. Clubbing all night and working all day was not for me. Amadu would come from the club by 5 am, have a wash, change and be at work by 6 am. That worried me a bit. I kept telling him it was not healthy and not safe, especially when he was the one driving, he needed a few hours' sleep. "Don't worry Or-Mrs, I will sleep when I came back from work," was his response every time.

I had spent about six months at McDonald's, but the wage was not as good as expected.

Still no pregnancy. Whenever I spoke to my mother, grandmother, or friends it was the activity of my womb which interested them the most. I went to the Tesco Express on Market Street one day and decided to get an application form. I now had six months' work experience that might improve my chances of working somewhere else. The manager told me they were recruiting staff. He gave me the forms and told me I had to do some test or exams online. If I passed the exams, they might call me for an interview. I filled out the forms and took the online tests or exams. They called me about two to three weeks later for an interview.

I went to work at McDonald's a few days after the interview with Tesco. One of the managers was having an attitude with me. I had no idea why; I just carried on with my work. By the end of my shift, she called me to the office. "Why do you want to leave us Christiana?" She was looking a bit unhappy. "Did we do anything wrong?"

"What do you mean am leaving, who told you that?"

"No one, it's just that Tesco called asking questions. I am the manager so I know you have applied or gone for an interview." I was truly surprised. So they actually called to check, wow!

"No am not leaving. If I get that job, I will be working there on weekends when am off from here." She finally smiled. As I was going out of the door she yelled, "You might get it." I did the fingers crossed sign and left. It was around 4:30 pm the next day when I got a call from Tesco asking me when I would want to start, and to not forget to bring my bank details. "I only have the joint account."

"That's fine with us, as long as it is fine with you," he said. I thanked him then hung up.

I would do 5 pm to 11 pm at Tesco. As soon as I finished at McDonald's, I would catch the bus from Burry New Road to Piccadilly Gardens then walk to Market Street. I would rush upstairs, put my bags down and start the evening shift at Tesco.

After the shift, I would try to get on the last bus to Littleton Road which left at 11 pm. The shift also finished at 11 pm. I would log out ten or fifteen minutes early to get on the bus. Because I would leave early they would then deduct about half an hour pay from my shift, but I didn't mind.

I had been doing both jobs for months now, and had been feeling very tired and unwell. It must be the work and the commute, I thought to myself. I phoned the general practitioners (GP) and told them how I was feeling. My whole body hurts especially my feet and my lower back. I went and they did some tests including a urine test. When I picked up the phone one day, I was chasing after a bus from one job to the other. It was the general practitioner (GP).

"You need to come in for more tests, this one shows you are pregnant."

"What?" I responded.

"Were you not expecting it?" she questioned.

I gathered myself quickly. "Am fine, when should I come in?"

"You can come in tomorrow."

The tests verified that I was about eight weeks or more pregnant. I had been so busy and had been barely thinking about pregnancy. Amadu and I had been drifting apart slowly. He would finish work at 12 most nights and would still not be home until 3 am. From his place of work to the house was about 15–20 minutes. He said he liked to go to other arcades to play or do whatever it was that they did there. When we were together at home one evening, I told him the news.

"The doctor says am pregnant." He just stood there. That was not the response I was expecting. After the shock had left his face, he came close to me and said, "Congrats Or-Mrs."

"Congrats Or-Mrs," I repeated, "did I make myself pregnant?"

"Come on, you know what I mean," he said.

"No, I don't." And I went upstairs.

The pregnancy wreaked havoc on my body, I could no longer juggle both jobs. I gave my resignation to McDonald's. The job there was too demanding on my body, I moved around and lifted things constantly. At Tesco, I just stood or sat by the tills all day. As a cashier, too much lifting was not involved. Only, working at Tesco now meant I didn't have to wake up at 4 am or 5 am and be home around 11:45 at night. My body was feeling a lot better.

I had my uniform on ready to go to work one day. As I was ascending down the stairs, I felt something warm on my legs. When I looked it was blood. I could not explain what went through my mind. I called 999, I was in pain with serious cramps. They told me to leave the door open if I could. They took me to the hospital. I phoned the office and explained what had happened. They did some scans, and the radiologist said the sac where the baby was, was intact. "The blood is not coming from the sac." He said everything was fine, it might just be the fibroids.

With five months gone I decided to tell my grandmother and everyone else. My grandmother was truly pleased. When someone was going to Freetown, I sent her some pictures of the baby bump.

After the scare of a miscarriage, I moved to the other room. My body did not want to be touched, I kept thinking it might harm the pregnancy. Another reason was Amadu would either wake me up with the alarm or when he came back from work or from his nights out.

One day out of nowhere, he told me we might have to move house. He said he was going to sell the house and get another one. "Why would you want to sell it, there is nothing wrong with it?"

"Or-Mrs, I just want somewhere more family-friendly."

"I don't want to move, I know my way around here now, this place is not too far from where I work." I stopped and turned to look at him. "Where do you want to move to anyway?" I asked him.

"Wigan," he answered.

"How am I supposed to get to work on the bus, it's too far? I don't want to move," I said simply.

"You don't understand," was his only response.

I didn't want to argue again, but my mouth was really itching to. As he went to sit on his Xbox I said, "When are you going to stop playing on that thing? You are not a teenager, stop acting like one." What I really wanted to say was stop going out all the time. But the words got stuck in my throat.

He turned and looked at me. "You want palaver en." And he turned his focus on the game again. With one hand he gestured. "Come and sit down."

"Just carry on, am going to lie down." I was six months pregnant and my back felt heavy when I walked or sat down for too long or stood up for too long. My feet felt sore, they were not swollen, they just hurt. I just felt constantly tired, all of the time.

He would come with me to the scans, but not to the other midwife activities. I told Amadu we needed to buy a few items for the birth and for the child, therefore I would need some money. I went to Mamas and Papas and got all the basic stuff: baby cot, pram, steriliser and some baby clothes. Joyce came with me to the shops, and we got all of the main things.

I was just over seven months pregnant when one day I came downstairs to get something to drink or a snack. Amadu was on the phone. As soon as he saw me, he ended the call, and his body language was shifty. "Who are you talking to at this time?"

I had never questioned him before. "It's one of the girls at work, they needed something," he said.

"So why did you cut off the call as soon as you saw me?"

He said nothing. It just felt odd, and I was feeling intensely stressed. I walked up to the bedroom and went to bed. At work that day I told my friend Isiah when she asked me what was wrong. I told her I thought he might be messing around. And she said, "Yeah but at least he is denying it. Do you know what my husband tells me?" She started speaking in a deep voice, "You made me do it woman, you are always stressing me out, you refuse to give me more children, all my mates' children are growing up, what makes you think am only going to have just one child." At this point, I was laughing so hard I thought I was going to piss myself. Then she stopped and said, "Imagine the idiot." As she concluded, we both started laughing again with tears on our faces.

"What do you say to him when he tells you that?" I asked her.

"What can I say to that Christy." That was what she called me. "I phoned his mother and told her, she told me to stop stressing her son. His father married five of them. I did not let her finish narrating, I just pretended it was a bad line and hung up." Isiah looked serious and said, "Am going to leave him."

"Are you sure, how are you going to leave him? Where will you go? Please don't make rushed decisions," I told her.

"Don't you worry Christy; I have already put a deposit on a bedroom. As soon as it becomes available am moving out of his house." It looked like she had made up her mind.

"Isiah, please think over it."

"Staff announcement: can Isiah and Christiana please return to the check out." Our names came through the speaker in the canteen. We looked at the clock. "Let's go, we are more than five minutes late."

That day I was so tired physically and mentally, so I slept on the bus, I could not get off at my bus stop. When I woke up, the driver was yelling last stop at Salford shopping centre. I called a taxi. The wait would be about thirty to forty minutes. It was dark and it was cold. Forget it, I said to myself, "I can't stand here for that long." There were a lot of teenagers running around. I just walked instead. My back and underneath my stomach had been hurting on and off all day, sometimes more, sometimes less.

I got home and Amadu was on his Xbox again. "Where have you been?" I told him how I had slept on the bus. "You should have called me," he said.

"I did not know you finished this early today." I walked past him. "I was not expecting you to be home at this time, I was expecting you in the morning hours." He did not say a word. I went to the kitchen and made myself a cup of tea, had a wash and went straight to bed. When I woke up to go to the bathroom, he was still on his Xbox. I was washing my hands when there was that pain again. "Amadu!" I screamed in panic and fear. My waters had broken.

"What can I do?" He ran down and grabbed his phone. "Stay there, don't move, no sit down." He called for an ambulance. Then I heard a voice on the phone, a few minutes later I was on my way to the hospital. "God please let it be ok, please save my baby. Where is Amadu?" I asked.

"He is locking up, he will drive behind us when he has finished," one of the emergency men answered. The pain was picking up speed now, then it would relax for a few seconds and intensify again. I could hear the paramedic saying the waters had broken and they said my name as they spoke to the nurses. They put me on the bed and one of them checked me over. She made a shocked face, and the other nurse came to look.

"Listen to me, you have to start pushing, ok," one of them spoke.

"No not now, I want the epidural, I can't push, please," I spoke back.

"Christiana, there is no more time to do anything, you really need to start pushing. The baby's head is already engaged, you are fully dilated."

I shook my head in defiance. "No, please no." But then I started to feel my own body pushing involuntarily.

"At the count of three now push." She coaxed on.

"No it is too painful." They brought gas and air. "What is this?" I asked

"Breathe it in, it will help with the pain." I did, then pushed it away with my hand, it was not doing anything for the kind of pain I was feeling, the pain was still there.

"Jesus!" I screamed as I pushed. "You said I should call on you when am in pain."

"Push! Push! Push! Push from below, the way you go to the toilet that is how to involuntarily push," the nurse kept saying. After I caught my breath, I waved for the thing, the gas and air. I took some more breaths; it made me a bit dizzy.

"Now push!" the nurse beckoned again. I was screaming the way I was feeling the pain, I was screaming non-stop with every strength in me, I was screaming the name of Jesus, I was saying all sorts.

The other nurse smiled a little and the other nurse said, "Shut up Christiana, other women are around."

"I don't want to know. I don't care if they can hear me, just do something, just give me something to stop the pain," I carried on talking.

The other nurse looked at me and said, "Take a deep breath and when I count to three, you push as hard as you can, do you hear me?" I nodded, one, two, three, push, Jesus! I screamed a very long and loud scream.

"Good, good, the head is out," she said, and then finally the baby was born.

They took him and wrapped him up. I couldn't hear any baby cries, what was happening? And then the cry came. "We need to take him now; he is six weeks early," the nurses discussed amongst themselves and then they left. A doctor and another nurse I had not noticed looked after me and I could hear them talking about the afterbirth, then they let me sleep.

By the time Amadu arrived the baby had been delivered. He looked surprised. "That was quick, where is the baby, what happened?" Too tired to speak I just looked at him and drifted off.

It did not take long until I woke up. A nurse came with a wheelchair. "Come on mom, let's take you to meet your son, he is now stable." Amadu was peering down in the incubator when the nurse wheeled me in. The nurse said, "Speak to him." And she pointed at the incubator. "He knows your voice, he can hear you."

He looked so tiny lying there. "Hello Treasure." Treasure was what my father's friends used to call me. They would call me Mr Kamara's Treasure or MAL Kamara's Treasure. That was the only name that came to mind at that point. We had not thought about names that much. "Your great grandmother was waiting for you," I spoke through the incubator. "My grandmother could not wait any longer, she died December and you are born in February. She really wanted to meet you. Is that why you came this early? Well you have missed each other." Amadu rubbed my head, the nurse wheeled me back to my bed and they spoke to me about what methods of feeding I was going to use.

"I will breastfeed him."

"Do you want to pump some milk so we can feed him when he wakes up at night, or we can wake you up to breastfeed him?" "Wake me up," I responded. They would wake me up at all times: 12 am, 2 am ,4 am. "The baby needs feeding mom." By the third or fourth day I started expressing milk and putting it the fridge so they could feed him whenever he was awake.

The next day, Amadu brought balloons, cards and flowers to the hospital. He told me he had remortgaged, or sold, the house in Salford. I did not say a word. I had known tiredness, but having a human come out of you in the most raw and natural form, I really did not know that type of tiredness. He would come from work, see us and leave. Some days he would bring his friend. We spent about twelve to fourteen days at St Mary's hospital in Manchester. I could have left two days earlier, but I had a little panic mode. I told the doctor and nurses I didn't know what to do with a baby. I had been around babies all my life; my mother delivered babies on a daily basis. I would hold them, play with them and give them back. What was I going to do with this tiny baby? I could not be in the hospital forever.

It was time to take Treasure home. When we got to the car, he had changed the car too, it was now an Audi TT. Why was this car so small in the back? It was uncomfortable and not child- friendly. If anything, you could have gotten a spacious car, I thought as I sat down. He drove us straight to Wigan; we never went back to Kersal Way in Salford.

We arrived late in the evening. The house had a garden in the front and in the back, it also had a garage on the side, same three bedrooms, so not much difference to me as I looked around. I went to the kitchen and noticed a new fridge; it was much more spacious than the old one. I opened it, and it was empty. My heart sank. "Where are the things in the old fridge?" I asked him. "The food items, what have you done with them?"

"I threw everything away."

"Why would you do that? I spent a lot of time cooking and saving that food stuff." He did not say a word. "It was for me to have something wholesome to eat when I delivered the baby." Still no word from him. "Especially in times like this." I had read about preparation in one of the pregnancy books. So, I had cooked and frozen food. All my cooking items, which could not be found in most shops, were gone also. "Why did you do that?"

He finally spoke, "I did not think about that. I just get rid of the fridge and got a bigger one. You can buy other food items."

"You should have asked me; you should have waited for me to come out of hospital at least."

"Just relax Or-Mrs, don't stress yourself out." And he left. All I did was shake my head from side to side.

He came back with some salty takeaway. I had a few mouths full and went to attend to the baby. The next day, he went to work, there was nothing else to eat apart from cereal, so I had some of the leftover takeaway for lunch. All that breastfeeding was making me eat more. I had to wait all day for him to bring food after work. I didn't even know where I was, it felt like when I had just arrived in the UK for the first time. I was reluctant to leave the house or scared to leave the house because the baby was so tiny to be put in a pram.

By late noon one day, I dressed the child and went out of the house, walked to the junction and entered the corner shop but there was nothing I could buy or wanted to buy. I asked if they had any Tesco or Asda supermarkets around. An elderly lady told me, as she looked at the baby, "It's a bit of a walk, all the way up that hill." By now she was pointing to the direction. "Morrisons is the closest supermarket around here, it's about a thirty-minute walk."

I thanked her and left, it was sunny and bright. A lot of people were moving around, that gave me more courage. I thought to myself, if anything happens to me someone will call for help. I was feeling a bit shaky still. Just a few days after I had returned home, I had had a lot of bleeding with heavy blood clots. A midwife had come to the house and told me I would be ok. When I got to Morrisons, I picked up a few things that I needed.

I managed to make myself something to eat in between feeding the baby, changing his nappy, and getting him to settle down. I spent most days alone. The midwife would come and showed me places to meet other moms, that was it. I would talk to Isiah on the phone, and sometimes I would talk to Joyce. Both of them came to the hospital on various occasions to visit us. But they had never been to Wigan. Joyce was at university and working long hours after uni. Isiah had taken all the overtime at work just to avoid her husband at home.

Weeks had passed and I was feeling a lot better, I had even discovered how to get to Bolton market. That market had plenty of fish and fresh produce. During one of my walks, a lady spoke to me about Avon. She said they needed someone in the area, she explained to me how they operate. I took the card and told her I would think about it.

Amadu was still going out with his friends and his shopping habits had not slowed down either. If he was not at work, he was at home sleeping or nowhere to be found. Around three months after I had the baby, I noticed he did not go anywhere for the whole day, he even took the baby out in the garden and asked me to take a photo of them together.

When the baby slept, he came and sat close to me and started talking, "You are still glowing Or-Mrs."

I sucked my teeth at him. "Is that all you came here to tell me?" I ask ed

"You know, it's been months and months now since you started sleeping in the other room."

"And so," I answered.

"You don't even look at me, it's all about Treasure."

"Yes, he is a baby, and you are an adult."

"Well, I need Mummy too." He smiled and pressed himself on me. I think my body just responded. He held my hand and took me to the other room. I was hesitant. He smiled again. "Don't worry, I will be gentle."

He told me he was going on holiday with his friend Mark. He wanted some of the money from our joint account.

"You should not use that money for a holiday," I told him. "You said we should save it; you are spending everything else." We had some big arguments and he ended up having the money.

A few days later they left for the holiday. I can't remember where they went. He called me to say they had arrived safely and that was it. They returned and everything was fine. He was going to work and coming back as usual.

I noticed he had not unpacked his bags since his return. When I was hoovering the whole house I lifted up the bag to make way for my hoovering. One of his pairs of trousers fell out, and when I picked it up a card dropped out. It was from a woman called Adina. It was a love note to Amadu, expressing her love for him and thanking him for the holiday which they had just spent together. The only way I could explain it, was, at that particular second, I felt the clamps not just on my feet, but this time my hands just got clamped as well.

He had to sign every document of mine for me to get my stay. Never mind my heart which had just been shattered. And please I did not want to be reminded about BB at this point, I was not in the mood. I was shaking, I had not put too many thoughts into that call the other time because he actually worked with a lot of women and they did call him sometimes, asking for stuff or to tell him stuff. But there was no doubt about what I was holding in my hands now.

As soon as he got home, I was waiting.

"You have not even told me how the holiday went?" I started. "Did you have a good time?"

"Yes, it was alright," he responded.

"It was more than alright I can tell, especially when Adina was there." I gave him the card or note. There it was, proof of evidence, he could not deny it this time. All he could say was, "Why did you go through my things?"

"You know I have never or will never go through your things, or your phone." Then I explained how I came into contact with the note and he was muted. I left him and focused on the baby. He got in his car and drove off. He came back a few minutes later with, "We need to talk, it is not what you think."

"My passport needs to be renewed; they cannot give me the two- year temporary stay on an expired passport," was my response. I did not want to hear what he had to say.

The following day, I phoned the Avon lady and started doing it with my son. I was still on leave from work. My maternity leave had started on the day I gave birth. "You will be dropping leaflets though doors and collect back the leaflets after a couple of days. If they make any orders, then you have to deliver their products." She explained it was going well. The only thing was that some houses had dogs inside and the dogs would bark unexpectedly. That gave me a fright from time to time. I needed to be busy.

Amadu came home one day after work with Mark. It looked as if they were going out for the whole night the way he was getting ready. I brought the papers down for him to sign. I was standing on the trying to block him from passing. He just shoved me instead. His friend came to pull me up, he told him, "Me man you can't behave like this." But I removed myself from Mark as he was trying to help me up. I knew Mark knew everything. In fact, it was when they had started hanging out together that his going out or behaviour became worse. And it was with him he went on the holiday. He must know who Adina was or knew about Adina. They left and he did not come home that night. It was a first, he would usually come home at four or five in the morning at least. I sat there at around eight or nine in the morning thinking maybe something must have happened to him.

I put the chain on the door so he could not come in. I was trying to stay safe. I refused to open the door for him. He stood there for a very long time. He was due to start work at twelve noon that day he told me. I did not take the chain out of the door until I knew the time for him to be at work had passed. When I finally opened the door, he was enraged. A little revenge can be so satisfying.

The arguments escalated from that time onwards. I phoned his mother, Aunty Isatu, and told her everything. She said, "He is your brother, that is how boys are, just look after him, talk to him politely, cook for him, you are not an in-law to me you are my daughter." Things had gotten so bad that I didn't want to be in the house, I was constantly thinking about leaving the house. But where would I go? How would I feed my son? How would I go back to work? They had stopped paying me, I was now on maternity leave without pay.

I told the midwife about how I was feeling. She suggested more activities and more groups. I told Joyce. She said, "Relationships are not easy, you have to be patient with him." I told Isiah and she said, "Please, whatever you decide, think about your papers and your son." Isiah told me her daughter was with her mother in Nigeria, yet she was finding it difficult after she had left her husband. Being trapped or stuck was an understatement. I had to do something, yet I had not a clue about what I was going to do, or what I was supposed to do.

I went to Barclays bank and opened my own bank account. I needed an account with just my name on it. That would be a place to start I told myself. Time to start taking full control of the money which I earned. I did not tell him anything about the new bank account. When I went back to work my pay would be going into it.

We had the nastiest palaver before I went to London. We had decided we could no longer live together. I went to the embassy to renew my passport. I spent almost a week with a friend Nata. Saudatu, I did not visit, I could not. She had warned me about Amadu, she told me not to move to Manchester, she wanted me to stay in London and sort my papers out. I did not want to see the "I told you so" in her face, even if she did not say it out loud.

I called Amadu and he told me he had found a place for now until things calmed down. When he picked me up, he drove to Lincoln Gate and told me I would be staying there in the meantime. I did not see that coming. I thought he was going to do the moving out, not move me out again. He had moved me without my permission once more. It was a bedsit; the kitchen, living room and bedroom were all together in the same place. The bathroom was the only thing that was separate. There was not even a toilet roll in the house or a kitchen roll. There was a bedbug-infested bed on one side and a two-seater sofa on the other side. I did not know bedbugs existed in Great Britain. My son was crying unusually one night. I got up abruptly and put the lights on. They were biting him, some of them were on the wall, they were everywhere.

How had it come to this? Within six months, I had lost two of the homes I lived in, I had given birth to a child, I couldn't go back to work, so I had just lost my job due to childcare issues, I had lost the father of my child. And the documents still didn't have his signature on them. Therefore, I was more or less with no papers. It was as though I had been pushed into a river with clamped feet and clamped hands. That was more than enough to send anyone into oblivion.

The midwife, on one of her visits, gave me a form to fill out. She was a bit concerned after I had filled it out. She said I might be suffering from mild postnatal depression. She went on to explain how plenty of women went through the baby blues. And my current situation was not helping. I almost laughed, this was not just the baby blues, it felt more like life blows to me, I thought to myself.

I started attending the baby groups again and made new friends. I could walk to my place of work from where I was now living. I got to see Isiah every time I was in and around the Market Street area. Seeing Isiah always lifted my spirits up a bit. Conversations with her would make me laugh so much until the landlord called for his rent. Then it was time for me to come back down with a crash-landing.

I had to call Amadu which in itself was like a self-stabbing. Now I had to ask him for rent money. The landlord always called me a week before the payment was due. He was always threatening to start the eviction process if I didn't pay the rent on time. If I was not with child, I would have called the immigration on myself in order for me to get deported. I had spent almost three months in the bedsit. The office called and told me they couldn't hold my place anymore, especially when I had not given them a specific date to return back to work. The six-month leave was over, the three-month extension I had asked for was also coming to an end. "How are you supporting yourself without the maternity pay?" the secretary asked me.

"There is still some money in the joint account," I said absentmindedly, not wanting to discuss the issue.

"Take this number down, call them, it is an income support number. They should be able to help you," she said in a soothing tone.

"I can't call them, you have seen my passport, I am not entitled to it, no recourse to public funds remember."

"You might not be, but your child might, just call them, ok. Take care of yourself Christiana." And she was gone. I put the phone down and finally broke down. My job had just gone and so was my self-respect. I was unable to console myself. I could only move to attend to the baby. Well, my appetite had gone as well. I had lost weight drastically.

Amadu would still pass by sometimes to see the baby. But he was still refusing to sign the papers. I had even threatened to call the police. One day I went to his place of work because the time to submit was getting closer and I was getting desperate and more stressed out. He would not even speak to me, all he said was, "I will see you after work this is not the place and time."

"You said that the last time and I did not see you," I responded and left. What would I do if the time ran out? That was my biggest worry. At first, I thought he was just playing mind games, or he was showing me who was boss, but it looked like he was never going to sign them. How would I get a job without papers? The "what ifs" came crashing in again, and this time, I didn't have the faintest idea of what to do. No plan B or plan C.

This was definitely not the stress-free life I had envisioned to be living in the United Kingdom.

One morning I finally took the courage to call the number which the secretary had given me. A woman took all the necessary information as she interviewed me over the phone. She asked me to take the child's birth certificate and other proof of identification to the nearest centre. She gave me the address, and I wrote it down. I explained this to Amadu when he came to see the baby. I was practically tired of talking to him about one thing or another. Some days I would not say a word to him. He would come in, spend a few minutes with his son and leave.

One evening he took the papers and said he was going to sign them when he got to his house. He wanted to go over them because he was tired and needed to go and rest. I did not hear from him the following day. I called around the time he usually finished work. He did not pick up.

The following day, nothing, I could not reach him either. What was he doing now? What was his game? I asked myself. How come his behaviour had become so appalling? I said to myself. When I visited his place of work again, he was more or less laughing or smirking. I could not take it any longer and called the police. I told them he had my papers and he was refusing to sign them or to give them to me. He had even threatened to burn them. I waited outside as they went to speak to him. He told them how he brought me to the UK, how he got me a lawyer and went to court for my papers, why would he not sign them, or why would he even think about burning them. He told the police he loved me, I was his wife. It was only a small misunderstanding between us. I was just stressing over nothing, it was probably because I had just had a baby. By the time the policewoman finished telling me what he had said, my mouth was open, and words could not come out. She went on to say, "Please, you should go home and settle it later, don't try and get him into trouble or get him fired." Wow, she had taken his side.

"You call this a small misunderstanding?" the question finally came to my mouth. Now what was I supposed to do? I was later told by Women's Aid that if I had taken the details of that officer, she would have had some questions to answer.

Because my move from Wigan to Lincoln Gate was sudden, I still had to attend all the clinics and appointments in Wigan. Our general practitioner (GP) was still over there. After the appointment, I waited at the bus stop for a long time, there was no bus. My son was crying, I suspected he might need breastfeeding and maybe a change of nappy. I went to the house in Wigan to feed him and change his nappy. I got to the door and put the key into the door. What was going on? It was the right key, I double-checked and tried again, nothing. It was at that point that I realised he had changed the locks on the door. That was a really uncomfortable and a bitter experience for me. It took me a very long time to get over that particular encounter and to be able to move away from such a bad experience. I sat at the side of the house to feed my child. After he was fed, I changed him. We got the bus back to Manchester. When trying to cross from Market Street to the other side of the road, to enter Debenhams, so I could walk back to my apartment there was a sudden yank on my back. It was two women pulling me so hard. I felt my body and the pram jolt backwards.

One of them was crying, she sounded Nigerian. "My daughter, what is wrong?" Then I heard the honking, and saw the tram go past. If they had not pulled me and my child away, who knows, I might not be telling this story or this narration. I was lost in all the confusions in my life, to the point that I did not see or hear the tram. I did not know what to tell the women. They spoke to me for a while, I thanked them and left.

I jumped in a black cab that was usually parked by the roadside. When I gave the driver the address, he looked at me strangely and said, "It's just round the corner love."

"I know, am just too tired to walk," I responded. About two or three minutes later, we arrived, and I got out of the cab then paid the driver. I could feel my nerves getting close to breaking down, if they were not broken down already.

The midwife advised me to see the general practitioner (GP). I had just registered with a new one at Cheetham Hill, which was the closest to where I now lived. The midwife was adamant that the doctors would be able to help. The doctor I saw on that day was a lady. After examinations and further questions, she said I should try some antidepressants which could help me. After a lot of conversation and thoughts, taking into consideration the stigma attached to antidepressant, I told her, "Yes, I would like to try some please, if they might help the way I am currently feeling."

She gave me a few. When I got home, I took one. A few hours later my tongue felt heavy, even my lips were heavy, my eyes had become drowsy. The next day I took another one, my speech was slowing down when I spoke. I phoned the doctor and she said I might be having a bad reaction to it, furthermore, it would take a week or two before the medicine kicked in or started to work properly. "If this one is not helping, we can change it and put you on another type of antidepressant." By the third day it was still having a bad reaction on my system. It was difficult for me to even lift the baby up. I stopped taking them entirely. They were making me feel worse and unable to function properly.

I started going to a church just across the road: the Manchester Cathedral. I made an effort to eat more and to eat well, I went for runs or long walks again, I was trying to sleep whenever the baby was sleeping. Slowly, my mood felt lighter and I started to feel much better again.

Amadu came one evening and he seemed to be staying around more than his usual few minutes. He was starting to behave well which was suspicious. I kept asking myself, why was he acting like that? That kind of behaviour was now a strange thing between us. He had come from work and would stay in my apartment until I could ask him to go because I needed to close the door and sleep.

After checking my account for more than the hundredth time, finally there was some money in it. I had made friends in church and at the baby meetings. Things were starting to get better and so were my mind and body.

I never touched the antidepressants again. I arranged for my son to be baptised at Manchester Cathedral. Joyce and her son came, Isiah was there, Amadu invited his friend from Norwich who brought his wife and two daughters, my church friend was also there. After the baptism we went to the bedsit and ate some of the food I had prepared.

When everyone had left that evening, Amadu stayed behind and helped me clean up the dishes.

Chapter 21

After seeing his friends off, Amadu returned to the apartment. I thought he had gone, but he came in and would not leave. He ended up staying the night. And he came the next day, he stayed the night again. I stopped talking about papers altogether. I was going to try and play his games. One day he brought the papers in an envelope, and we went to hand them over to Aziz the lawyer. He was to verify them before they would be sent off.

After posting the papers, I felt relieved and even better. The dark cloud was slowly being replaced by a bright and blue sky. I went out with friends more, one of my old friends came to visit me from London. She brought her son who was about a year or two older than my son. We visited Blackpool for the day. We took so many pictures and got the train back to Manchester.

The time went by quickly. Some days I felt like Amadu and I were getting closer again and on the other days it was as if we were on opposite sides.

But I had finally decided not to waste time thinking about that any longer. When my passport came back with two years' stay, I decided to go to Freetown to see family and to just have a break from the non-stop emotional turmoil. It was time to think about the next step, or it was time for me to take the next step. I told Amadu what the plan was. If my son adjusted well, I would want him to stay with his mother. I told him to buy the ticket for his son and I would buy my own ticket. Treasure was less than two years old. His ticket was not much, but he just paid the full amount anyway. The months before I left, Amadu was spending more time in my apartment and sleeping there. He was still acting like nothing was wrong, and nothing had happened between us, as if we were still properly together. I was so unhappy about the situation between us. I had no control over it. I was existing on a coping mechanism, just letting things take their natural cause. If I talked to my friends, they would say, "You have already gone too far, just wait for your passport." I was still afraid or felt like it was wrong to go out with someone else even though we were not together properly, yet again, we were still together, sort of. It was all so confusing to explain it to myself, let alone to explain it to anyone else. Was he incapable of recognising the damages his actions were doing? Or he simply didn't give a toss. Sometimes, it was a tug of war in my head, trying to process between what he was doing and how he was not affected by everything. Both actions had a negative effect on a human's health.

I was looking forward to seeing Freetown and family. Salomi my friend, and Baio, my younger brother, picked me up. Rugea was still working at the airport, so everything went well. We were really happy to see each other. They were more excited to see Treasure in particular. Amadu's younger brother picked us up after we had crossed from Lungi airport to Government Wharf.

I stayed with Amadu's mother. It was a full house, everyone was there. I told his mother everything that her son had done. But that kind of thing was trivial and to be expected from some African men. That was more or less what I got from her and from her reactions. She said she would pray about it because bad people were the reason for her son's behaviour. They must have been using some kind of *juju* or black magic on her son, "married os to scater".

My aunt was pleased to see my son. As soon as she saw him, she started crying and her daughter Cici FA joined in. They said he looked just like my father. They started calling him by my father's name. My aunt was always warm and welcoming to me in particular. The way she talked to me was just soothing and it always calmed me down. Sometimes it felt as if she was talking to her elder brother. I went out a lot, mainly visiting family members.

My mother was not there when I arrived. I had sent massages for her to come so she could meet Treasure. I had no intention to go to her latest station of work at that time, not with my son anyway. I asked my brother and he had already told me that getting to where she was now working was either on foot or on a motorcycle, what we called *okada*. Okada were known for their fatalities. I was not going to risk my son's life.

It was almost a week before she came to Freetown. She took one look at me and said, "You are pregnant." I laughed. "Am serious," she said.

"It can't be, I had my period about two months ago."

She continued saying, "You could be almost two to three months gone."

I did not pay any attention to it. Before I came to Freetown, I already had a job with an agency. The manager to my new job was called Olaf. It was a new restaurant which they were going to open just around the Piccadilly train station. It was called Cotton House. We were to start just after I returned to Manchester. Pregnancy was the last thing that was on my mind. My mother spent about three days with us and returned back to the village.

I left after two weeks and also left Treasure behind. I was ready to go back to working full-time. For the first few days at work in Cotton House, all we did was offload drinks from the van to the store, clean the coffee machines, learn how to hold the plates, what side to serve the customers, and from which side to clear the plates. They gave us some pamphlets on a brief history of the wine. We had to know at least where the wine came from, what year it was produced and so on and so forth. More again, we should know a little bit about what kind of food the restaurant was serving. The uniforms was a black skirt and white shirt with black shoes. After a few days of setting up the place, and putting everything in place, it was time to finally get started. The day it opened, the restaurant was full. There were a lot of family members and friends who came to support the owner with the opening. He introduced us to his wife. The wife took a whole table for her and her friends. They looked happy to be there, drinking and eating all evening. Everything went well on the opening. When most of the guests had left, we cleared the tables, emptied the plates. My shift was 5 pm to 1 am. The working environment and the job were going well.

When I was not working I missed my son terribly. It was a struggle to cope without him. He was almost two years old and how do you communicate with a two-year-old from thousands of miles away? I could only go by what his aunts and grandmother were telling me. I would call my brother, cousins, friends to go and check on him, or to go and see how he was doing. All of that did not help, everyone gave me a different explanation.

At work it had been almost a month now and we had not been paid. Olaf kept telling us they were trying to sort everything out since it was a new business. By the second month two members of staff left. They said they were not going to keep working without getting paid. I left as well by the third month. Not only because of the payment issues, but I was finding it difficult to hide my pregnancy. I was almost five months gone when I handed in my resignation.

I left my bedsit and moved to a two-bedroom flat which was owned by a woman from the church I was attending. The flat was just off Strangeways prison. The rent of the bedsit apartment and the two-bed flat were more or less the same price. The flat was clean, safe and decently furnished. As soon as I received my paycheck from Olaf, I cashed it, bought a ticket to Freetown and brought my son back with me.

It was almost eight months before I got offered a flat by the council. I was on the waiting least for over two years. The day of the viewing was another experience which I was not prepared for. The house was completely empty, not like the bedsit or flat I was now living in. At least they had beds and cookers and chairs. I stood there with the council officer, not moving or knowing what to say. It was completely empty. It had no carpet, paint, or wallpaper. There was not even a cooker, absolutely nothing. Within two weeks I had to make a choice: to decline the offer or to accept it. If I declined the offer, they would either remove my name off the waiting list or I could go back to the bottom of the list. The housing officer looked at me, noticing the confusion on my face and he spoke, "You wanted a house, now, you got it."

"It is quite some house indeed," I answered.

He then told me I could apply for a moving-in loan, but would have to pay it back interest free. After the viewing I accepted the house. It was a maisonette house; another house was on top of another house, which made it look like a block of flats from the outside. That was the best way I could explain it. Mine was on the ground floor. There was a garden that looked like it had never been used, or as if there was some mining taking place there. Some parts of the ground had massive gaps in them. The ground was uneven, and the bush was overgrown and thick.

I gave notice to the landlady who was now one of my best friends. I was a bridesmaid at her wedding at the same place where I had my own wedding. And I signed her wedding certificate as a witness. "Just when I thought my bridesmaid days were over," I told her laughing when she asked me. After church, we would go to the food court at the Arndale and we would get something to eat. Some days she would invite me to her house, where I met her fiancé for the first time. When I gave her a sudden notice, she was not happy about it, especially due to the short notice. She said I would have to pay for the whole month. I thought she was my friend. Well there was no friendship in business I should know that. My stress levels were starting to increase again, I was almost entering the last months of the pregnancy. There was some money saved which I was going to use to buy stuff for the empty house. Now I was going to be paying a whole month's rent because I was contracted to give a month's notice. That gave a dent in my pocket. I couldn't move my son into the house in the condition it was.

I was determined not to ask Amadu for anything anymore. We were no longer on speaking terms. It would take weeks before I would have a word with him or see him. That was only if and when he wanted to see his son. He would pick his son up outside the house and drop him off outside the house. He did not come inside the house anymore.

The new empty house needed carpet and wallpaper at least before I could move in. I checked my savings, and it was a bit descent: a few hundreds of pounds. In my place, they said if you knew how to shop for food then you knew how to cook. Something like that. It went, "Who-dat sabi buy buy E sabi cook." I knew how to buy, and I could cook and store food that would last us for a couple of days. I was not eating out anymore or buying lots of stuff. My shopping was mainly food and clothing for my son.

I went to the shops in Cheetham Hill and they gave me someone to go and take the measurements for the house. They needed to know how much carpet the house would need. It was at that time when I noticed the lack of curtains for the windows. I went back to the shop owner and gave him most of the money I had and told him I needed the carpet, wallpaper and blinds for the whole house. "It should be good quality and fairly priced."

He laughed and said, "Yes, all customers want good quality but don't want to pay a good price." And we both laughed at that statement which was mostly true. There was only a bit of money left for me to pay him and he said not to worry, I should pay him back when I can. "I know you are not going to run away when you are pregnant like that." I laughed again because I was getting bigger every day.

A friend gave me a local handyman's number, whom we simply called Mr T. After he gave me the cost of putting up the wallpaper I did not know what to say. It was way more expensive than the wallpaper itself. I said that to him, and he said, "Ah, why do you African women always say the same thing?" I was lost for words. "Of course putting up the wallpaper is more expensive than buying the wallpaper," he said cheekily.

"Please calm down Mr European," I told him. And there was another round of laughter. I gave him a deposit and he started the job at once. He said, "You are lucky. I am on a holiday from my main job, there is not much work for me right now. I will start as soon as possible, ok."

"Fine by me, Mr European, please do it well and do it quickly, I have a deadline to move in."

"If you don't mind me asking, where is your husband?"

I just smiled and said, "Long story." Then I gave him the keys to the house.

I called him every day to see how far he had gone or if he needed anything for the work. By the time Mr T had finished the loan came through. It took almost a month to organise the move. The landlady took my deposit for the one-month notice she needed. Well, I might as well spend the time getting myself organised. After paying everybody off, I now had to get a van and man to move us. I did not have much left to buy a cooker, that was my main concern now. We moved in, Mr T did a good job, the place looked bright and liveable.

It was a cold winter evening when we moved in. I tried to put the heating on and it would not come on.

When I called, they told me I should have been the one to call and notify them about my moving in, so they would have had the gas or heating activated or something. It took about two to three days before the heating issue was fixed. They gave us tiny heaters the following day.

For us to eat, we would take the bus and go to Cheetham Hill for dinner every evening to buy cooked warm food. We were living on fast food and takeaways until I had had enough, then I bought a cooker, and then a bed.

When Amadu came to visit his son, he was surprised. "Who did the painting for you? he asked, standing in one of the rooms.

"I did it myself," I responded.

"When you are that pregnant?"

"No, when I was sixteen years old," I answered.

He just shook his head. We called that kind of answer "back talk" in my place. In English it was referred to as sarcasm or something of the sort. "It's a bit of a risk don't you think?" he continued questioning.

"How is that any of your problem? I like painting walls, am fine," I spat the words at him and left the room.

He was still living in Wigan and by then I had sort of gotten used to our separation. If he wanted to see his son, I let him, no more, no less. Seeing his face made my blood boil at that point in time. I was starting to finally see what he had put me through. And the fact that I was pregnant again was not making it any easier. All the fuss about the papers had made me look at him differently.

He asked if I needed anything for the house. "Am fine, all I need is a cot for the baby," I answered. I could deliver any time by then. It was the last days of the pregnancy. He bought the baby cot, and a few clothes. I had a hospital bag on standby. This pregnancy was less stressful than the first. I did not have any scary trips to the hospital. I had gained a lot of weight compared to the first one though.

I was to give birth on 26 December but my son did not arrive until 30 December. He was almost 10 pounds; this birth was even more painful and difficult then the first birth. The drama and screams I did with my first child doubled the second time around. I said to myself, God please don't let me go through this pain again. There was bleeding after I had delivered, but the doctors were finding it difficult to locate where it was coming from. I could hear them discussing it amongst themselves. I could hear the anxiousness from their voices, the sense of urgency, or a bit of a panic that was apparent. I knew I was drifting in and out of consciousness.

We returned home just after two or three days. I needed help with Treasure and my newborn as my body healed and recovered. There was no one to rely on. Everyone was busy with their own lives. They would come to visit, spend a few hours and they would leave you to it. I had no choice but to let Amadu help with the boys. My body was physically aching. He would come by after work or sometimes on his day off. He would look after the children while I slept or just had a rest so my body could regain the energy it needed. Those were the times when I really wished to be with my extra-large family.

Looking after the boys and looking after myself was not an easy task, definitely not as easy as it looked. There were no breaks, it was constant, there was always something to do, somewhere to go, the shopping and so much more. I went from the independent single mum who wanted nothing to do with their father, to asking him to spend time with them whenever he could. Sometimes he would have them while I went for a walk or a run, that thirty to sixty minutes I just spent with myself were like little gold nuggets. I learnt to look after myself, it helped me look after the boys better.

Whenever Amadu came in for a few hours, I would make sure he ate before he left. That was because I wanted him to spend more time with the boys. He looked like he was having a good bonding time with them, but you never knew what the little rascal had up his sleeves. He could easily say he had something to do at work. I was very careful to not piss him off.

Until one day I left him with the boys and went for a run. I would go running all the way to Heaton Park. I came back, had a wash and decided to use the computer, I wanted to quickly check on social media before he left. As soon as I clicked on the mouse, I was taken straight to a Facebook page which was not mine. I saw all the conversations: they were between Amadu and a woman. I did not even know he had a Facebook account. That was the first shock, so I wanted to know more. I decided to pretend it was Amadu, she responded immediately. By the way I was sending the text she knew it was not him. The second shock was when she asked me why and what I was doing with her boyfriend's Facebook page. I did not know if I should convulse or combust. "Composure, oh composure". I took deep breaths and typed, *well, your boyfriend just happens to be my husband whom I had two children with.*

She said, *that is a lie, we work together and am always at his house. He only has one son.*

Well add three more to that and now he has four altogether. I think it was her turn to not only be shocked but to collapse or crawl down from the high horse because there was no reply for a moment.

Just as I was about to get off the computer, she replied asking for my name. I told her my name. She said, *yes, I have seen your name in his phone, I believe you.*

How funny I said to myself and wrote back, *look miss, I don't really care if you believe me or if you don't believe me. I have no reason to make all this conversation up or even have a conversation with you. A few minutes ago, I did not know you existed.*

She gave me her name and it was definitely not Adina. I said, *he is in my house right now, helping with the children and he is using my computer to chat to you, my dear you are more than welcome to him.*

I unfriended her and logged off; that was my little revenge for him chatting to his girlfriend in my house on my computer. I turned around and saw someone I did not recognise. Every time it was a new low. "Yes, we are separated but you could not even care to log off. What was so pressing that you couldn't wait, how could you be so disrespectful and so heartless, what happened to you and Adina or are you seeing them both?" I was trying my hardest to keep my voice down and to be as calm as possible.

He was confused at first so he said, "What are you talking about?"

"I am talking about you using my computer to chat to your girlfriend in my own place. Why don't you just bring her with you next time." Complete silence. "You work together don't you, she told me everything." He could not say a word, I said to him very calmly, "Please just leave now. You are not setting foot inside this house again. If you want to help with the boys, pick them up, your girlfriend can give you a helping hand, I don't care, just bring them back in one piece."

"Please Or-Mrs, don't look at me like that," he finally spoke. "Just get out before I do something really stupid." My body was in pain, I didn't know if it was from the run or from what I was experiencing. He left without saying a word. Whenever he could he would pick the children up.

My mindset had automatically switched up again. It was now me and my boys and my mindset was once more in survival mode. This was not the time to be getting rests, or quick naps or just having time for yourself. From now on, when they rested then I rested. When they woke up, I woke up. That was the way it was.

When my first son started to go to school and spent the whole 9 am to 3 pm at Crab Lane Primary school, I decided to enrol at Manchester college. I got a place at the college and a nursery place for my younger son. The day of the entry exams, I had to bring him to the classroom. One of the teachers played with him in the pram when he woke up. Thank God he did not scream the place down.

Chapter 22

The bus from the house at Bridgnorth Road to Manchester college was every thirty minutes. I would drop off one child at Crab Lane primary school, which was less than a five-minute walk from where we lived, then catch the bus to the college. At the college I would quickly drop my child off at the college nursery and then make my way to the classroom.

I did not know what to expect on the first day. I had left school a very long time ago and also did not know how the other classmates were going to be. When I got to the class, it was a surprise because most of the other classmates were just like me. Some of them looked like me and sounded like me. The majority of them had children, some of the women and men had their husbands and wives, and like me, some of them were separated, divorced or unhappily together. Some were still happy living together though.

By the end of the class, we got to know each other a bit more and that put me at ease. All the subjects on health and social care I could understand, except for maths which I just had a phobia of, but was still trying my best. I would spend hours doing my coursework. When the children were sleeping I would do the research, find books at the library, or use internet links. Then I spent my time on them. If I was not reading the books, I was on the sites. Soon my class tutor Carol took notice. I was not showing of I promise. I only answered the questions when she asked me directly and I would always try to give her an answer or sometimes too many answers and she would say, "That is for the next topic Christiana." "Oopsy or is it woopsy?"

Another time Carol asked us to write an essay about an incident involving the police in our area. I did not have to think too much as we such incidents took place near us on an everyday basis. One of the men living at the top of the house was a dealer of either cannabis or other drugs. I had seen his exchanges and dealings with his customers. Sometimes when I was putting the bins out into the communal bin, there were needles on the floor or the smell of whatever they were smoking was apparent. I didn't know what transpired between him and the other men who usually came to visit him. All we saw was his motorcycle going up in flames. The police were called and the area was closed off. In class Carol gave everyone their essay back, but mine. Then she took the last one on her table and said, "This is like anything I would read in a newspaper, the way you have explained it." With a tiny smile I collected it. One of the girls shouted, "Are you trying to make us feel depressed?" We all laughed. And another one said, "I can sense the favouritism Carol." We laughed again. "Does my essay affect you?" I responded.

"Ok ladies, pay attention." And we continued.

That motivated me and distracted me and completely took my mind away from Amadu. Sometimes I would even forget he existed. I had formed close friendships with some of the women especially Leticia. Her younger son, Yohan and my younger son were best friends at the nursery. We would sometimes meet up in Piccadilly Gardens and then go to the cinema or go to a restaurant. She convinced me to go to France with her for a few days. I told her it would cost a lot because I had been to

Disneyland with the children and Amadu and it was a bit costly. She said, "That is because you took a plane and stayed in the hotel at Disneyland."

I said, "Yes how else are we supposed to get to France if not on a plane?"

"We take the coach and then cross with the ferry," she responded. "If we leave Manchester in the morning, we will be in France very early the next day." I was just looking at her as she explained it. "But it is not good to bring the children. Just the two of us." She took out her phone, typed something and showed me the dates and cost. I felt the sense of adventure warming and hugging me. I said, "Go on, let's do it."

But now I had to ask Amadu to look after the children for a couple of days and I was not sure about that. But she reassured me, saying she had left all of her three children and they were fine. I called Amadu and told him about our little trip. He was a bit apprehensive. I told him it was fine, I just needed him to look after the boys for a few days. He could stay at my place or his place, wherever was more convenient for him. He agreed.

I was planning to celebrate the boy's birthday and I wanted to do something special for him. Leticia said, "France is the best place to shop for a party." She was soon telling me about kids champagne and all sort of party food, she told me about wines and more. She said, "We should take empty suitcases."

The day of the trip we met up at Victoria coach station in Manchester. We got on the coach with my two empty suitcases. We sat next to each other and we chatted all the way to London. When we got to London a friend of Leticia's met us at the coach station. Then the three of us left for the other coach station to France.

We checked in, took our seats and she waved us goodbye. She was a very friendly lady. It was a long trip; we would talk, fall asleep, wake up and start chatting again.

After a long drive, I was woken up with loud sounds of honking and the sounds of sea waves splashing. Leticia told me we had to get down for our documents to be checked. We were in Dover. We got in the queue which said EU citizens. Our documents were checked, and we got on the ferry. It was a massive ferry; we went to the canteen and got some warm food and some hot chocolate. Travelling on the ferry for long hours would always leave me feeling a bit light-headed. Thankfully I did not get seasick.

We had travelled all day and night. By the morning around 5 am we were in France. I was so glad to walk on land or to stand on my feet again. Leticia's uncle and his wife picked us up from the coach station. We drove for just a little under an hour before we arrived at a block of flats just around the corner from the Stade de France stadium. We took the lift and got off at the fourth floor. They showed us around the flat and showed us our room. I went straight for a wash then crashed on the bed. It was around one in the afternoon when Leticia woke me up saying, "Christiana, wake up, let's go and eat lunch, we did not come all the way here to sleep did we."

"You are right woman." I sat on the bed laughing sleepily. I got up, brushed and we had lunch. The hostess was a good cook I thought. The first thing we did was walk to the Stade de France stadium to have a look around, we took a few pictures. Then the three of us got on a bus and then a train and arrived at some marketplace which was packed with all kinds of things and produce. But the thing that got my attention the most was the riot police holding guns and some of the gun men were going up and down with the guns in their hands. I asked what was going on, if there was a problem. And she simply said, "Not really, it is always like this." The police were covered from head to toe. I took one more glance and all I wanted to do was tell them to back off. We got a few items and continued to walk around. The marketplace reminded me a bit of Africa where my aunt used to sell. They were even selling roast corn on the fire coal. We bought some from an elderly lady and it tasted really good. It was good for just the three of us women to go around shopping and having a laugh. We were behaving like teenagers. Since I had phoned Amadu and told him we had arrived safely, I had barely given them a second thought.

The next day we carried on with the buying of our party items. The third day we visited a family from just outside the city. They were having a barbecue, it was enjoyable. We all sat outside on a very big table eating and telling jokes or stories. One of the men was telling us about his friend, who had a bruised rib. But his friend could not go to the hospital because he was too embarrassed. His friend had gone to Africa and got himself a wife. The wife would refuse to have sex with him. Every night when his friend would reach out and try to touch the woman, she would use her elbows on his ribs to try and get him off. It had gotten so bad, yet he could not explain himself to the doctor. The way the man was gesturing, the facial expressions and the accent, by the time he had finished explaining, everyone at the table got to a feast of laughter.

After stuffing our faces, we left in the evening and went back to the house. We did our last rounds of shopping and packed our bags. The bags were now bursting out with all kinds of kids party items. We had to drag the bags to the lift the following morning. We left France very early in the morning and embarked on the same long trip to Manchester.

Chapter 23

"What the hell do you have in these suitcases?" Amadu exclaimed as he picked the suitcases up. I did not respond to him, I was hugging and talking to the children. When we got home, I noticed his work clothes and a few of his items in the room. It was interesting how the human brain just switched back on to where it had left off. One moment I was carefree in France and now I was back to motherhood with full force.

I washed the children, got their dinner and put them to bed. I came down and sat on the sofa watching *Coronation Street*. I was waiting for Amadu to pick up his stuff and skedaddle. Instead he came and sat next to me. "You should go to France more often Mrs, you look calm and relaxed. I have not seen you like this in a very long time," he blabbed on. I knew what he was up to, I knew his game by then. I just turned around and gave him a strange look then smiled suspiciously. He was going to take advantage of me it was visible. Or he wanted to take advantage of me. But the truth was, at that moment, I was prepared to participate in his game. "Are you not going to work in the morning, you should go now? And thanks for looking after the children." He smiled and planted a kiss on my lips. By the time I could shove him off, my body was embracing him. Well, "it just happened", as they say. He left from my place to work the following day.

I started prepping for the party, I got the invites and started distributing them. I gave some invitations to the women and men in my class and gave some to my children's school and some to the church I was now attending.

I told Joyce and she said she would help me with most of the cooking. She told me what she needed and I gave her the money to buy the items.

The day of the party I woke up very early and started cooking. I cooked every party food I knew how to cook. I even made pepper soup. Amadu arranged for a DJ to play. Bukky, a friend in church, came to help and she brought some puff-puff cakes, she also brought more plastic chairs for sitting in the garden.

By the afternoon the guests started to arrive, and before I knew it the place was packed. Thank God for the plastic chairs outside. "Christy, where did you get all these people from?" It was Isiah from work. I laughed and said, "Everywhere, college, school, church and so on."

She brought her daughter from her new relationship. Her daughter had grown up so fast. I remembered visiting her in hospital when she had just given birth. She was not expecting the couscous I cooked for her. "Christy, you have to show me how to cook this thing," she said to me as she was eating it. And we certainly discussed that ex-husband of hers. I wish he could see her and her daughter now, I thought.

The guests enjoyed the food and the music and drinks from France. There was a lot of laughter and dancing going on, the children somehow got upstairs, and the adults naturally took over their party. At least they enjoyed their kids champagne and the cake.

Joyce, for what every reason, decided to pass the cooking onto someone else. She did not notify me about it. I had spoken to her almost every day. Maybe she forgot to tell me. The drama of it all. I called to see when she would be arriving with the food. It was then that she said, "It is too far, I got my cousin to cook the food for me. Please tell Amadu to come so we can go and collect the food from my cousin's place." I tried my best to contain my dissatisfaction. By the time they arrived half of the guests had gone. The food she brought was cooked well though. Some stayed till the DJ packed up. It was around one in the morning before I got to bed. The party was sort of successful, thank goodness.

It was the end of the academic year. With great efforts, I got my level 2 Diploma in Health and Social Care. Getting to college and doing the school run was not making the experience stress-free. I was always late to class, sometimes I would miss the bus by a few seconds, then I would have to wait for another thirty minutes or more before there was another one. By the time I would get to class I had missed half of the lesson or a whole lesson. And I would have to leave the class at least half an hour early or I would be too late to pick up my son from school. There was no after school or breakfast club for his age group. It was a marathon from the time I got up in the morning till the evening. I made up my mind to learn how to drive, that might significantly reduce the distress of the everyday commute; it was getting too much to catch up on the lessons every day.

I would go to the teachers so they could give me more explanations. Some did and some would not. One of the teachers told me, "I can't explain the whole lesson to you again, you have to ask your classmates." Which I would do sometimes. But the way they understood the lesson could be different from the way I would have. Leticia finished at level 2, she said that was enough for her. I started attending the level 3 classes for the first term. By the end of the term, my eldest son, Will got conjunctivitis symptoms or something that looked like conjunctivitis. It was around spring. His teacher said it had been going around in their class. I took him to the hospital, and he recovered.

A few weeks later my younger son, Chris developed the same symptoms. By the second day I had to rush him to A & E, the eyes had become so red and he was struggling to open them. They gave us some eye drops and referred us to Manchester eye clinic at St Mary's hospital. He was around four years old. The eye drops from accident and emergency didn't seem to be making much difference.

During the referral at St Mary's, the doctor took a look at his eyes, and then called other doctors who came, took a look, and another doctor was also called. They decided amongst themselves that he needed an operation as soon as possible. The doctor said he was going to try and get hold of some placenta which he would use to put over the eye after the operation. Then his eye lid would be stitched together until the eye settled down. He said he would then give us different eye drops for his eyes. We agreed and signed the consent forms. By that point, Chris was now struggling to do the simplest things like playing outside. He simply could not open his eyes if the lights were on, or if the place was bright outside. The sunlight was painful in his eyes. Going outside of the house was almost impossible. That was the end of Manchester college.

A few weeks later we got an appointment for the operation. I held his hand as they put him to sleep. It was like someone had gotten hold of my heart and was yanking it away. Amadu was there as well. After they took Chris away, I started praying every prayer I knew. I refused to think about anything going wrong. The operation took longer than the time they gave to us. Then finally, they wheeled him in. The doctors explained that everything went well. We stayed with him until he recovered. The doctor said it was keratoconus or an eye ulcer.

When we got home, I turned my attention to the house again as the damp had taken over the rooms. I was not sure if it was the cause. Sometimes I thought maybe it was the damp. I searched for why and how this was happening to the boys. The wallpaper was now peeling off the walls because of the damp. The damp was on the clothes at the back of the wardrobes; it was impossible to get rid of. I tried every anti-mould product I could get hold of. I used anti-mould paint and painted over it, but after a few days it would spread like wildfire.

I called the council and explained the situation to them. After a series of calls, they sent someone to come and investigate. He brought some kind of instrument, and he used it to point at the walls, and it would either beep or flash a light. After a couple of times pointing it around the house he concluded it was not damp. He said it was condensation. I told him from what I could see, it was definitely damp, I even peeled off some of the wallpaper and showed him but he was adamant with his report. He told me to open the windows more, that would help. And I told him I opened the windows every day. That was it, nothing was done about the damp; according to him it was no damp anyway.

Chris recovered from the operation. There were a lot of eyedrops to put in his eyes and sometime the teachers would forget to put in the drops or maybe they were too busy. So, sometimes I had to go to the school to put in the eye drops or phone to remind them.

I discussed the damp situation with the doctor and he said they might need to run some tests to see what he may be allergic to. He was allergic to pollen, some pets and house dust mites. I scrubbed the house every day just to be on the safe side or to avoid any dust. The appointments were regular because they had to monitor his eyes. They would have to see Chris most days in hospital and by the time we would get back from the hospital, I would have to call Hanna, my elder son's best friend's mother to pick him up until I could get him from their place.

Our life had changed just like that. Chris had a third operation, and they injected him in his leg every three months especially during the summer when the pollen count was very high. The injections in his legs would help to contain the symptoms within those three months. They gave him drops to put under his tongue every day. Things calmed down a bit, but any time the seasons changed the symptoms would re-emerge again. The doctor said it was going to be like that until he grew out of it; when he was in his late teens it would get better. He said reassuringly that the symptoms would subside by then.

Once I had familiarised myself with my son's condition and its challenges, I set myself to get us out of that house. The second damp investigator that came after the damp had engulfed the house told me to close the windows more. He said leaving the windows open for that long might be the reason why the damp was getting worse. He just contradicted what the first investigator had said. "The other man said I should open the windows more," I answered. Yet again nothing was done.

I started job hunting; I was attending a lot of work-focused groups. I got my CV updated and applied for any job that was within my time frame. I went to plenty of interviews; the time was always the hindrance. One of my interviewers said to me, "That time you want, 9–2 is like gold dust, every parent wants to work within those hours. Even if we have that space, it will be for the ones who have served us for a long time."

I eventually took a night shift at Asda. When the children were sleeping, I would go to work from 10 pm to 6 am. I worked on weekends, Fridays, Saturdays and Sundays. I was not going to the hospital every week or every other day anymore. The injections in Chris' leg were proving to be effective.

Amadu was leaving the house one morning after he had looked after the boys when he asked me a question, "What have I done Or-Mrs?"

I said, "Why, what is it? Are the children ok?" I had just come back from work, all I wanted to do was to have a lie down.

He responded, "Yes, the children are ok. Am talking about you and me," he carried on talking, "this is pointless, I have been young and stupid, I can't let you carry on like this anymore. I am giving up my flat, am going start looking for a place so we can move in together."

Here we go again, was the only thing I could think of at that point. He was not living in Wigan anymore, he was now living somewhere else. "What makes you think I want to move in with you?" I said to him.

"The children," he said simply. "It is too much on both of us, paying bills on two houses, and looking after them, it is all too much."

"I am tired, we have been doing that for years, let's discuss it later." And as he was walking away, I said, "Don't you think for one moment I cannot get another man."

"Yes, I know that. I remember how guys used to crash their cars when they saw you," he said teasingly. I sucked my teeth then rolled my eyes and we both just got into a feast of laughter. "Am going to bed before the boys wake up." And he left.

I did attempt to go out with other people but, it turned out that they required more than I could give or was able to give. They did not understand the situation with my children. I intentionally refused to bring anyone near the children. I hardly had time for myself. One of them wanted us to go out on the weekends, well I was working on the weekends so that was that. Another one wanted to chill, just do what normal individuals in a relationship do. But my situation was never normal. I had boys who needed extra care. They were not "special needs", they just needed more time and effort with everyday activities. I told them straight what the deal was. One guy said, "My stepfather raised me, you got to allow yourself some fun." But fun was not part of my vocabulary at that stage of my life. I lost fun a very long time ago. There was this one who was always asking me out, by insisting he come to my place for lunch or dinner. Not a chance, I would reply to him. What is wrong with the boys in Europe was a regular question I often asked myself. When I was in Africa, I thought the boys in Africa didn't know how to treat a woman or how to be with a woman. I assumed the boys in Europe would be more civilised and more proper or more honest. How wrong was that idea? According to my experiences and those of my friends, there was more or less no difference. A human is a human, sometimes the environment does not make much of a difference on the behaviour. It is all about what the human has within them.

On our bus route, around Cole More Drive in Blackley, they had just started building houses to be rented out. I went there and made enquires, I got all the details I needed and showed them to Amadu. We needed to raise a deposit and about two months' rent, plus a guarantor, proof of work, proof of previous address, the tenancy agreement of a previous landlord and so on and so forth. Until you got those items, you were not guaranteed a reservation, the agent told us. It took us over three months to get everything that was required. By then, most of the houses had gone.

We managed to secure one of the houses on the last plot at Cole More Drive. And in December, after Christmas, we moved in on the day of my second son's birthday. It was our Christmas present and birthday present for that year. We did not buy any presents for ourselves; we had saved up every penny to get that house. The children got their own rooms for the first time, and they cut a birthday cake in the house. The smile on their faces would never leave me.

I gave the keys back to the council and wondered if they would fix the damp properly, or if maybe they would just whitewash it and then rent it out to the next unsuspecting tenant.

The new house was more spacious, it had its own inbuilt wardrobe in the main room, a built-in dishwasher, the kitchen was modern, the garden was also a good size, flat and levelled. So, I bought a trampoline for the boys, and got a shed on one side of the garden. I had always liked to entertain people, be it friends or family. I bought a barbeque at Tesco and invited a few friends to come over. Well, maybe more than a few. Everything went well, we lived there for almost two years, and everything was going well.

Then Amadu lost his job. It was a shock to us all, the management he worked for sold up within weeks and left everyone in limbo. We managed to survive for three months on his redundancy and my pay before we were totally depleted. I got paid monthly and it was impossible to get all the little things done. Everything was about to crash land. Amadu was a lot of things, or could be a lot of things, he could even be a complete cow but the only thing that was for sure about him was he could work himself to death. I would always say to him, "You need to make more time for the children."

To see the pain and frustration in his eyes was excruciating. I applied for working tax credit, told them everything. It took weeks before it came through. Once again, everything we earned, we saved up to pay the rent. I was in the car with him when I heard an announcement about Payment Protection Insurance (PPI); I knew he had used a lot of credit cards in the past.

"You will be eligible; in fact, this is your area," I said to him laughing.

He said, "That was a long time ago Or- Mrs."

I went and got the forms anyway, I coaxed him to fill out the forms and I posted them for him. He was truly surprised to get a response. We filled the forms out again and sent them off. He was by now training to become a truck driver which was really expensive. He was still actively looking for employment, he would even do some security job here and there. He said to me that if the money actually came through, he was going to start his own business. He said he was tired of working for someone else, which was a good idea, I supported his endeavours.

The money came and he started working towards building his own business. He bought all sort of things, some days I would go with him to buy the goods. He got a container and shipped them to Freetown, Sierra Leone. A few weeks later he left for Sierra Leone with the hope of selling everything. After he sold his goods, he was going to use the money to buy diamonds or gold and sell them in Europe. That was the trade of his father. His father was some big diamond digger and seller in Kiodu town. He left me with five hundred pounds.

After a few weeks he called and said he needed some money. I send him all of the five hundred pounds. To cut a long story short, he came back, went through Dubai and the human could not tell me a thing about the business or the money. Why did I let him back into my life? This man would never learn, he would continue to take advantage of me for as long as I let him. He had done it so many times. We would save money, he would take it all, and I would not even get an explanation. With all the financial constraints we were going through, he went and came back with nothing. I could not even look at him and I didn't want to argue in front of the children all the time. I told him to look for somewhere else to live. It was two years since we had moved in for the second time, but we just could not make things work between us. I was fed up with the can't completely be apart, or the can't completely be together. He did everything he could, he even brought his friends to talk to me, but there was nothing he could say for me to change my mind.

He left and everything else went just like that. I started having debt collectors come around the house asking for him at some point. They would come first thing in the morning before the children even went to school. That really scared me off. I phoned him and told him. As usual you would never get a straight answer from him. I asked my manager at work and started doing some overtime. I needed the extra money to keep things going. After a few weeks I received a letter from the tax credit, saying I should pay back a substantial amount of money due to the overtime I had been doing. I was soon getting court orders and added fines for late responses which added to the already huge bill they said I owed. Every day, some bill, or something arrived asking me to pay for something. I could feel the stress in my throat and could even taste it on my tongue.

I was now spending more time at the gym with a couple of friends, we became close quickly. I did not tell them anything about my personal life. We laughed a lot and went to most of the classes together. The gym was my "escape". Some days I would be at the gym until it was time to go and pick up the children from school.

And one day there was an announcement through the gym. They were advertising about personal training courses. Working all night and sleeping most of the day was chipping away at me. I asked the manager at the gym, Marc, and he explained to me what to do and the payment process. I could do the payments by instalment. I enrolled and started doing the course. I got myself so busy with work, the children's activities and the PT course, yet the problems of my relationship and financial troubles hung over me constantly. Every day the mail arrived I would feel the full force of fear in my brain. Court order after court order. I spent a lot of time on the telephone trying to fix things, but all they would do was pass my phone call from one department to the other. It was affecting my sleep. I already didn't sleep at night due to work, and during the day I struggled to sleep due to life stresses. How could I unbind myself from the constant financial woes that were always crashing on my brain like sea waves?

Chapter 24

I picked up the phone without even looking at the screen. It was a familiar voice, my friend from Birmingham. I had most of the letters in front of me, most of which had not been opened. "Are you ok, you don't sound your usual self?" For the first time I told her about the problems with my tax credit overpayments. She knew about Amadu but not all the details. She explained to me that when she was having problems with her husband, she had some assistance from some women until she was able to stand on her feet again.

You should call them; she gave me the name of the organisation. "Search for their number and give them a call they might be able to help or advise you on what to do. Just call them," she insisted. After a week I researched the name on my phone: Women's Aid. I got the number and rang it. A woman picked up and I explained myself to her from the relationship with Amadu to the debt collectors and the tax credit. She told me she would discuss it with her manager and they would call me back. They phoned me back saying they had a space, they could take me and the children in, but I would have to come to Birmingham. They said I could stay with them until I was able to sort myself out.

I told the lady I would think about it and call them back. A million things were going through my head, the children's school, their football practice, the house which they loved so much. We had paid almost two years rent. After two years we would be eligible to buy the house using the rent we had paid as a deposit. How could I just leave it all behind me? It was almost

Christmas, the voice of the woman I had spoken to kept cutting through my head. "We don't hold places, there is only one space left." What would I tell the children; how do I tell them? I kept asking myself. It was bad enough that their father had left the house, but at least we were in the same town, he could see them or they could see him. But to relocate at such short notice was going to affect them one way or the other.

I went to Manchester arena, which had just been bombed during a concert show. I could not believe if seeing it on the TV was different. I got a teddy bear and took it to St Ann's Square and laid it on the other flowers. It was one huge pile after another pile of flowers. People just stood there trying to process how it could have happened. I came back to the house and called Amadu. I told him I was leaving Manchester. I told him where I kept the keys and that he should give them back to the landlord and if there was anything he could keep or store from the house, he should.

Then I told the children we were moving. "You know your father has moved out and I am having lot of problems with bills. I really need a break and a fresh start so we have to relocate," trying to not let my voice break, I told them.

"When are we going?" they asked.

"First thing in the morning we are getting the coach."

I packed their football kits, a few things and we left. I phoned their schools and told them that the boys were not coming back. When we got to Birmingham, we were shown to our flat. It was a single room with two bunk beds and a wardrobe. The living room had a small blue three seater and one single sofa chair. The kitchen was within the living room almost. The bathroom was a disabled bathroom. As one of the women took the boys to show them around the house, I went to the toilet and started scrubbing it. I was trying to distract myself from thinking. I went to clean the bathroom when the lady who was showing the boys around came and told me she was taking them to the corner chippy to get them something to eat. She asked me if I wanted anything. Eating was the last thing on my mind. My stomach had closed completely.

They came back and ate their burgers and chips. After they had eaten, my younger boy looked at me and said, "Mom, what is this?" The look on his face before he could say the words is something I don't want to remember. He said, "Mum, you have ruined my life." The agony from his face and the words struck me like thunder. I felt like needles had pricked my heart. The surrealism was palpable, I tried to flee from the emotions I was feeling, I didn't want to break down in front of them. No matter what I did the pain tore at my soul. I restored myself quickly and hugged him. "It is ok Chris, we will not be here for ever, I promise." And my elder son came and also held him as he sobbed. My heart was smashed up, and I felt the full force of the decisions I had taken. It was unravelling as I held my boy, my nerves fluttered nervously. There was nothing more I could do, there was no going back. I felt every pain, every shame, every disappointment, every regret and they were slowly ripping through every cell in my body one by one.

In a couple of days, the boys seemed to be adjusting bit by bit. Thank God for the inbuilt adaptability which children generally have. We applied for schools for them; in six weeks they would be going back to school. Once they got back to a routine and got back on football teams and football practices the pressure would slowly evaporate. When they were in school, I would do my personal training work, I would attend the practical classes with others and I would pay for the course by instalment.

I was also finding my way and getting to know Birmingham, I was adjusting. At the flat the workers called the tax credit office, and, after a lot of discussion, we came up with a payment plan. All court proceedings were put on hold as long as I kept up with the repayments.

I also became close with some of the women in there. There were a lot of women from various walks of life and for different reasons. In the evenings, we would exchange stories and make each other laugh. We would go out shopping together and do Zumba classes in the main living room. Between going to the gym, studying and taking the boys for their own activities, the days were passing fast, and I had no time to think about what I had left behind. The only healthy and healing thing to do now was to look forward and to constantly reassure myself that I would once again pull through with the grace of God. I could not concentrate on anything else but the boys and the personal training studies and my mental health or my total well-being.

I submitted everything for the level 2 personal training course and passed the theory. I had to go over the practical. Then I did the level 3. I had completed the course in almost a year since I left Manchester.

I then turned my attention to getting my driver's licence. I also passed the theory, all that was needed was to do the practical. I found a driving instructor and took lessons once or twice a week.

The housing application was finally accepted, and it was time to start bidding for our own accommodation. Things were gradually going our way so to speak or moving in the right direction again, sort of. It was the second Christmas with Women's Aid and the children had adjusted, we all had. The children had lots of presents and activities and food.

Just after Christmas I started viewing and bidding for houses online. There was a two-bedroom flat. They offered it to us, and I accepted it; it was not what I wanted but I wanted to get out and stand on my own again. There was always someone to talk to or upload all your stress to in there. I said to one of the workers, "If I don't get out of here soonest, I will find it difficult to live on my own again."

"You will Christiana, I have no doubt in my mind about that," she responded and went on to say, "Most women have the same worries but somehow, they manage to find their own way in the big wide world. And you can always call us, remember that." Now it was time to really start all over again, carpet and flooring, curtains, beds etc. I painted the whole flat before the flooring was done. When I moved in, I was using the duvet cover as a bed.

I got an interview in one of the pure gyms at Beaufort Park Birmingham and got the job with them. I failed my practical driving test two times and passed it on the third attempt.

The boys had to move school again. I even got the social services or social worker contacting me, asking questions about why the boys had moved schools so many times. One of the teachers saw how many schools they had been to, she told the principal, the principal called social services. I spent hours, different days, explaining myself.

They told me they would get the police involved for further investigations and I told them to go ahead. That was just another drama, another bump, another glitch in my path which the children and I eventually crossed, thankfully with no casualties. Losing the children to social services would have been the last straw to break the camel's back. The day I was moving out of the shelter, the only significant thing I brought from Manchester was my 55-inch television, and it slipped from my hands and dropped as I was trying to move it through the door. The only thing that was keeping me company had now shattered. When the children were in school the new flat felt so empty and quiet, or maybe I could say it felt tranquil, to put it positively. The boys had their Xbox or whatever they called it, so they didn't watch television that much. Gradually we got beds, chairs, a fridge and all the everyday stuff we needed.

"Mum, I am still struggling to see the board in school," my elder son, Will reminded me. I had taken him to Specsavers and they said they would do a referral, but it had been over 4–6 months and still nothing. Another couple of months passed, I went there again, and asked one of them, "Please, are you sure you sent the referral? I have not received anything yet."

A kind lady said, "Yes, wait, let me check for you." She printed it out and showed me the letter they had sent. All we could do now was wait. I rang the hospital and they told me they had received the referral. They said we should wait for an appointment. It took about a year before we got the appointment. The doctors in the Birmingham and Midlands eye centre said it was too bad now, the only thing they could do to try and save his eyesight was to do cross-linking. More appointments and months down the line he was scheduled for an operation on both eyes. They did the cross-linking in the morning and we came home the same day. They gave us all the eye drops.

By the third day we were sitting in the living room and he had a lot of tears or water coming from one of the eyes. It was on a weekend, on a Sunday, he was not in pain so I waited until Monday morning and then took him to the hospital.

When they were looking at the eye in the machine, I could tell immediately that something had gone terribly wrong. As soon as one of them mentioned the word perforation, my chest tightened and I was struggling to breathe. Before I could contain myself, I was inconsolable. One of the eye surgeons put her hand on my back and gave me a tissue. The doctors said he needed a transplant immediately. He was thirteen.

He was admitted and told not to eat or drink hours before the procedure. He was given the anaesthetics and was taken in. When they came out the doctor told us that everything went well. He had pains in his stomach from not eating for a long time and when he ate the cramps were painful on his stomach. He eventually settled down. The nurses had to put the eye drops in every hour, all through the day and through the night, to prevent any rejection from the eye transplant.

Three years on, he could see well in the other eye if he used his contact lens. They decided the eye with the transplant could also have a contact lens, so he started using it and everything was fine. He would put it in before school and take it out after school.

He went out with his friends to the park one day, he came back, went to bed and when he woke up in the morning the eye with the transplant was swollen. I immediately took him to accident and emergency, it was around 20 September 2021, and it was on a weekend. They gave us some drops and told us to go back the next day. If you went early, you had a chance of being in front of the queue, there was no specific appointment time. The next day, they looked at him and noticed that one of the stitches had become loose which had resulted in the eye having an infection due to a leakage which was passing through the loose stitch. The loose stich was removed there and then. I couldn't tell if he was in pain or just discomfort; he was digging his feet on the floor and squeezing one of his hands into a fist tightly. The doctor noticed and put some more norming drops in the eye, he then relaxed a bit.

He was not admitted; I had to take him to the hospital every day to have his eye monitored. The doctors told us they didn't want to risk it or take any chances or there might be a rejection of the transplant. They gave us different eye drops: the eye drops had to go in every one hour both day and night. I set the alarm to wake me up every hour. Sometimes I would not hear the alarm when it went off. I tried everything to stay awake: lots of tea and biscuits during the night.

A few days later the eye calmed down and that contact lens was taken to the lab for further investigations, and he was told not to wear the contact lens for a while. He still couldn't see the board without his contacts, the glasses were not making much difference he told me. The teachers were understanding. A few weeks later the eye was better.

On 24 December 2021 we went to the contact lens appointment, and he was given another contact lens. He even put the contact lens in himself.

I also took Chris for his appointment and his doctor said his eyes were looking good. Apart from the scaring, there was no cause for concern. His eye drops were reduced, the doctor said I should now be putting the eye drops in every other day but, if anything changed, I should put the drops in regularly or take him back to the hospital. There were some days when the eyes would look a bit red or slightly swollen but there had not been anything out of control for Chris. No further appointments were booked for him. That could only mean one thing, the doctor was satisfied with what he had observed or he was happy with the way things were mapping out. Fingers crossed and touch wood I prayed to myself.

Will had his appointment six months later with the clinic at the Birmingham eye hospital. The doctor told me that the children's condition was not common but it also affected a lot of children all through their teenage years. It just happened to affect both of my children. It was not anything, anyone would get used to, but I now knew what was to come or what could be expected or what should be expected. My eldest son's eye drops had also been reduced to once a day. We had one of the best Christmases I could remember, both boys were well and in good spirits. They even had the Christmas present they requested from Santa.

I spoke to Isiah on the phone one day, and she told me her ex-mother-in-law was still insisting she return to her ex-husband. She now had four children in total. She said they had moved to Bolton in a bigger place or her man was doing business there.

I still had not given up the dream of going to university. I had been accepted at the A University and would be starting on 21 February 2022.

Amadu and I were on good speaking terms or in a good place. I had decided to not hold bitterness within me. I would never forget, yet I was not focusing on the ugliest parts of my life. I had learnt how to move away from a bad experience. He was now a delivery man; he made deliveries from Manchester to Birmingham almost every day. He saw the boys often. And he still called me Or-Mrs or his Mrs, well technically I still was because I had not gotten round to officially divorcing him yet. I had made enquires. "The case is very straightforward," the adviser told me. I didn't know how things would turn out, but no one knows precisely. All I was praying for was that God would give us the "endurance" to persevere. Would I ever be able to lead a turbulence free or normal life? Only time would tell. Does anyone ever get over the death of a close family member? I didn't think they could, they could only accept the fact that they were gone and learn to live without them. The only thing I could tell you was that unexpected things could stumble upon a human when they were not even looking or yearning or expecting. And every one of those could have a vital role in my life, be it significant or small. I was completely debt free, I had paid back every penny, I would never leave all my financial affairs in the hands of another human being again. I had lost count of the number of times I had moved from place to place or the places.

Now I knew not all individual's intentions could be the same as their actions. I was still a very trusting individual, not just as much as I used to be.

After writing everything and reading over to make some corrections, I made a few phone calls explaining that I wanted to publish a book. I was directed to the site to upload the manuscript. Then I started thinking to myself, do I really want individuals to know all this information about me? I spoke to my son about the second thoughts I was having, and he said, "Mum you spent so much time writing the book, just get it published." I was still restyling with the idea as to whether to publish or not to publish.

Chapter 25

On 5 February 2022, my elder son turned sixteen, and he was so excited to join the gym which his friends went to. It was on his second day at the gym when he said, "Mum, my eyelid feels heavy."

I said, "You might be tired because of the gym, go to bed early and get enough sleep."

He agreed. When he woke up in the morning of 16 February 2022, the eye looked red, a bit swollen and tears were running down endlessly. I decided to take him straight to the Birmingham and Midlands eye centre. I phoned the school and left a message for the student absence recorder.

The doctor looked at it and told us another stitch had become loose. The stitch was removed, and he said there was no infection. He gave us a prescription for some eye drops and some tablets for the pain.

We came back home with a follow-up appointment for the 17 February 2022. It was an 8:30 am appointment, but we were seen around noon due to the volume of people. The doctor took a look and called the doctor who had seen us the previous day. He asked her a question, and she said, "No, that was not on the eye yesterday." They told us to go and wait for the Conair team who would be in the hospital around 1:30 pm. I left several messages on Chris's phone to let him know I would not be at home when he returned and that he should stay with his friends. The doctor called us in again. By this time there were three doctors present. One of the doctors checked his notes on the computer then wrote something down on a paper and left. He came back and said, "The eye has been infected and we are going to admit him in the hospital so the drops can be administered every hour both day and night." There was a parch inside of his eye which was definitely not there the previous day. It was even visible to the naked eye. We were told to go to the waiting area and wait for the nurse to make all the necessary arrangements for the admission. I looked at my son and he looked fine, I held his hand, I needed his support and calmness. I squeezed his hand and he looked at me and nodded. "You worry more than me mum, it is out of our control, there is nothing we can do, it will be fine." I broke down, how was he so sensible. I called Chris and he told me he had got the messages and hoped Will got better.

The nurse came and asked us where he wanted to be admitted. She said that because he was sixteen, he could be admitted to the adult ward instead of the children's ward. She went on to say that being in the adult ward might increase the chances of the treatments getting started early. I looked at Will and he agreed to choose the adult ward. We were handed over to nurse Aleen to take a covid test, she took us to another room and another nurse did the swabs.

At 3:27 pm we entered the lift and got out on the first floor, we walked down a long corridor and arrived at his ward. They took my son into the ward and asked me to wait outside. I sat on the seats just outside of the doors. By 4:15 pm I buzzed on the doors just wanting to know what was going on. I spoke to the nurse on the ward and she told me they had taken him into his room and they were doing his paperwork so they could start the treatments. "I need to be with him," I said simply.

She looked at me with a puzzled face and said, "No, only the patient can come into the wards because of covid."

I panicked. "Is he is going to be all on his own? You mean no one will be with him."

"We are here, we will take good care of him, Mum," she reassured me in a calm and respectful tone. "But if you are not happy about him being in the adult ward, I will take you back down so he can be transferred to the children's ward." I thought about how long all the paperwork would take for him to be in the children's ward so I could be there with him. I asked to speak to him, and he came to the door. I explained the situation and he decided to stay in the adult ward. He went back to his room.

I left the hospital around 4:35 pm so I could get him the things he might need for his stay in the hospital. By the time I arrived home, it was 7:22 pm. The traffic was too much. I phoned his father and explained to him when the eyes had started to get worse. He came to help. I told him to stay with Chris while I rushed back to the hospital. Will told me he had had dinner, but the treatment had not started yet. I spoke to the nurse again and she said they were waiting for the doctor to log the treatments in before she could do anything. The first eye drops went in around 8 pm. I sat with Will, spoke with him for a bit and I left, got home at almost 11 pm. I checked on Chris, FaceTimed Will in the hospital; he told me he was not feeling sleepy. It might have been the change of environment. "It is going to be fine darling remember that."

He said, "I know Mum." Then we said our goodnights and hung up. I had something to eat and went to bed.

My meeting was at 2:15 pm the next day on 18 February 2022. I was going to cancel so I could go and see Will. But after FaceTiming him in the morning, he told me to go to the meeting and see him after the meeting. I went to the gym and did thirty minutes on the cross trainer. I went to the supermarket and bought a few items then made him his favourite pasta. By the time I had finished cooking the pasta it was almost 2 pm. I had a quick wash and changed clothes. I called a taxi and went to the meeting. I had not done any rehearsal or preparation, but the manager gave me positive feedback.

It was almost 4 pm when I saw my son again. He ate the pasta and was smiling in a satisfactory manner. I saw him every day, FaceTimed him as often as I could. On one visit he said, "Am fine mum, I just feel locked up being in the room all day. And I miss the gym with my friends."

"It will be ok, let's just focus on you getting better for now my dear, then you can get back to your everyday life, ok."

He nodded his head in agreement. I spoke to one of the doctors on 20 February 2022 and she reassured me that Will was responding to treatment positively. On 21 February 2022 he texted me; *I could be discharged today.* I texted back and said, *Good news* and we FaceTimed. At 1 pm, he told me to come and get him. I went to get him, but his medication was not ready; the nurse said the medicines should be ready around 6 pm. At 6:51 pm the text came in again; *the medicine is here*, followed by a picture of the medicine and a FaceTime call. At 8:41 pm Will walked through the doors of the flat. He was looking so tall and really grown up. The bacterial corneal ulcer was under control. He had four different drops and they could only be put in during the day; he could sleep through the nights again. He had dinner and went to play on the PS5; he chatted to his friends like he had never left.

After the last episode with Will, I decided to finally publish my little life story. It might just give someone the courage to carry on. I was to start uni on the day Will was discharged but I could not; I had missed the inductions and first day of university. I was hoping to catch up. I was at the reception of the university trying to sort out my emails, password and ID card when the phone rang on 22 February 2022. I excused myself to answer the call. It was the nurse from the hospital, she was calling to confirm my son's follow-up appointment on Thursday, 24 February 2022 at 1:30 pm. After we finally accessed my student emails, I got the timetable and my next class was also on the same Thursday at 1:30 pm, so I was going to cancel. Then, I called his father and explained the situation. He said it was fine, he had taken a week off just in case, so he would take Will to the appointment while I attended the first class.

Fingers crossed, I touched wood, I signed the cross and everything that could be done to not prevent me from going to class. I intended to be there around 12:30 pm. You never knew. I may even get a cup of tea or a cup of coffee as I waited. On Thursday when I got to the university, the classes were merged with a Manchester tutor online. Our tutor was on a leave. I joined the class online and worked on the induction modules on the laptop then came home.

The report on my son was good. I took both of them to the local shopping centre and got them a few bits and bobs. Will picked up his gym bag and went to the gym that evening. He had a wash when he came back from the gym, then he had dinner, played a bit on his game and went to bed.

Around 4 am on 26 February 2022, I was awakened by my son. He was calling my name. The urgency and pain in his voice made me sit up at once. "My eye, it is stinging." He had his hand over the eye that was hurting. I made him lie down on the sofa and took a look. It was red and swollen. I brought through the drops from the fridge and started to put them in hourly. We could not sleep. Around noon he settled a bit and got some sleep. I continued to put in the drops.

Sunday there was not much difference, so I made him breakfast and took him into hospital. There was no standing in the line on that day because it was not busy. We arrived by 11 am and by noon the doctor had examined him and looked at his notes. He said there was a 50/50 chance that he would need to be admitted again. "Am going to speak with the consultant." He came back with a scalp and did some scraping on the eye. A covid test was taken and in less than a week since he was last discharged, he was admitted again. The drops were administered just after the covid test was taken before we even got to his ward. Around 2 pm on 27 February 2022 the nurse took us to the ward. It was the same ward: room eight. One of the nurses jokingly said, "Did you miss us Will? How are you mum?"

I smiled and said, "It looks like he was missing you."

"Bless him," she responded.

Will said nothing, he just went to the room; he already knew the room on the first floor of the Sheldon wing at the city hospital in Birmingham. I had a discussion with the nurse in charge and had some conversations with Will then left the hospital. It was a bright day with a lot of sunny spells.

I got home, had some almond nuts and went to bed. I had not had a two-hour sleep in almost forty-eight hours. It was 4:20 pm when I got up that afternoon. I just had about a thirty-minute nap. Will was still looking restless and could hardly sit up or speak.

On Monday I was at his bedside around 10 am. We spoke a bit, he slept a bit and around noon I told him I was going to uni.

I sat in class and greeted the other classmates. There were nine of us on that day: seven women and two men. There were some students who joined in online. At just after 1:30 pm, our tutor Klara walked in. The discussions gave me a few moments to focus on something else. Klara was engaging and not rigid or too strict.

After the class I went back to Will in the hospital. I knew Chris would be going to play football after school with his friends. Will asked me what I did in class. He almost caught me off guard as he asked me some specific questions. I had to bring the notes out to explain what we did in class on that day.

He said, "I think you can do it Mum."

"Well, I intend to give it a good try sweetheart." I smiled at him and tapped him gently on his leg.

A few moments later I left the hospital again; it was raining. When I came home, Chris and I had dinner and we FaceTimed Will in hospital. "Mum, the doctor has removed another stitch again this evening, and the water has stopped coming out of my eyes. I am starting to feel better."

"That is the spirit baby, hang in there," I said to him.

Indeed, when I saw him the next day, he looked better, his mood was also better. "Have you done your homework?" he asked me.

"Not yet." I told him I was still doing the induction modules. "You should do it soon you know; it is important."

"Sure, I will do it, I promise."

When I saw him on Tuesday, 1 March 2022, he was chattier and even laughing again. Was it the jollof rice I had brought him or was it the fact that he was recovering again? But when I saw Will the following day on Thursday evening, he was not in a good shape. He could barely sit up straight, he was sneezing, restless and told me he was feeling feverish. I didn't know what else to do. They gave him some paracetamol and he went back to his bed. I was constantly thinking of him and praying for him. On Friday late morning he called me. When I picked up the phone it was his doctor. The doctor told me they had decided to take out all of the thirteen remaining stiches. He called to notify me that he was giving the consent form to Will to sign. They would remove the stiches in about a month's time when he got better. He said the way things were looking, my son might be home later on that day. I was already on my way to the hospital when I got a text from my son: *Come at 7 pm.* I arrived just a few minutes to seven.

On 25/02/22 he was discharged. Nurse Barbra explained to me carefully how to apply the medicines. One of them should be kept in the fridge and should be used every two hours, another one should also be used every two hours. There were two more which were to be administered four times a day and the last one, two times a day.

As we got in the car, I asked him what he would like to eat for dinner and he said, "Kebab."

"Kebab!" I repeated and we both laughed. "You have never ordered a kebab before."

"That is what I want to eat." He was being assertive. We stopped at Chelmund's fish and chip shop and we got one cod, one haddock, a portion of large chips, gravy and the kebab. We sat down and ate. I had always ordered the cod but for some reason the haddock, which I pinched from Chris's plate, was really crunchy that night. Their packaging was different to any other fish and chip shop I had bought from. They put the fish in a cardboard box, separate from the chips. We could not even shake the chips. Five people could not have finished those chips.

On Sunday 05/03/22, I took Will for a follow-up appointment. It was a 10 am appointment. The doctor advised that we continue with the same drops and at the same time intervals. He said Will should stay off school until he saw him again on Thursday, 10 March 2022. He gave him a note for the school.

The school, Grace Academy in Solihull, was always supportive. They would phone to check how Will was doing and the school would ask if there was anything they could do to help with his studies.

My son is almost back to being himself now. He is moving around, talking, playing and eating. Today we are even watching the Manchester derby. It is a Sunday evening of the fifth March 2022. So far, it is Manchester City 3 and Manchester United 1. It is eighty-six minutes and twenty-two seconds into the game. Will has got up and disappeared to his room. We both are supporters of Manchester United. I am disappearing to make dinner before the VAR confirms the fourth goal by City. Chris, who is an Arsenal supporter, is finding Manchester United's predicament amusing. At least one of us is happy.

Mr Turay told me one time, "My dear, the only time you don't encounter problems or the only time you stop dealing with problems is if you are not alive. Some problems may be more, some less. We must learn to endure."

The respect and appreciation I have for the health care profession is something I don't even know how to express. Without them, I really don't want to think of the various outcomes for the boys. I will always be grateful.

As I left the hospital that afternoon, both of us were in a much better headspace. We are hoping for him to go back to school and back to his everyday life as soon as he can.

Most individuals are trying to get out of a comfort zone or out of their comfort zone. Me, at this point in my life, all I am trying to do is find that comfort zone so I can spend some time in it.

For my children Will and Chris, you filled my life with joy, courage and a sense of purpose. Your love kept me safe, sane and kept me going.

I love you more than any words could say, may life treat you well. Your mother, Christiana.

CK King

Lightning Source UK Ltd.
Milton Keynes UK
UKHW011949270622
405049UK00002B/49

9 781803 694146